An Allergy Mom's *Lifesaving*
INSTANT POT® COOKBOOK

60 Fast & Flavorful Recipes
Free of the Top-8 Allergens

Megan Lavin
creator of Allergy Awesomeness

PAGE STREET
PUBLISHING CO.

PAGE STREET
PUBLISHING CO.

Distributed by Macmillan, sales in Canada by The Canadian Manda Group.

23 22 21 20 19   1 2 3 4 5

ISBN-13: 978-1-62414-760-9
ISBN-10: 1-62414-760-7

Library of Congress Control Number: 2018962310

Cover and book design by Meg Baskis for Page Street Publishing Co.
Photography by Megan Lavin
Cover image © Megan Lavin

Printed and bound in China

Instant Pot® is a registered trademark of Double Insight, Inc., which was not involved in the creation of this book.

To my sweet children who have these food allergies,
may there someday be a cure . . . and until then
I promise to always keep cooking for you.

Contents

Introduction   6
Things to Note Before You Get Cooking   8

Get a Move On Mains   II

No-Stir Stir-Fry   12
Honey Garlic Chicken & Broccoli   15
Sweet & Tangy Pineapple Chicken   16
Healthier-for-You Orange Chicken   19
No-Butter Indian "Butter" Chicken   20
Sweet Barbacoa   23
Chili Lime Chicken Tacos   24
Quinoa Nachos   27
Tomatillo Pork Tacos   28
No-Cheese-Needed Ragu   31
Bread Crumb– & Egg-Free Italian
Meatballs & Spaghetti   32
Tuscan White Bean Quinoa Salad   35
Creamy Italian Chicken & Pasta   36
Greek Lemon Chicken & Potatoes   39
No-Soak Red Beans & Rice   40
Shellfish-Free Jambalaya   43
Creamy Rice-Milk Cajun Chicken Pasta   44
Dripping Balsamic Pork Roast   47
35-Minute Herb Crusted Turkey Breast   48
Apricot-Glazed Pork Chops   51
Sun-Dried Tomato and
Greek Herbed Roast   52
Classic Sunday Roast   55
Chicken Taco Salad   56
Vegan, Nut- & Gluten-Free
Mac 'n' Cheese   59
Smothered Pork Chops   60

Stress-Free Sides 63

Cilantro, Garlic & Lime Rice & Beans 64

Lemon Herbed Quinoa 67

Salsa Mexican Rice 68

Dairy-Free Garlic Parsley
Mashed Potatoes 71

Cheese-Free Scalloped Potatoes 72

Wild Rice, Cranberry &
Sweet Potato Pilaf 75

Dairy-Free Sweet Potato Casserole 76

Southwest Black Beans 79

Bacon & Brown Sugar Baked Beans 80

Sesame-Free Hummus 83

Thick & Creamy Refried Beans 84

Honey Cinnamon Carrots 87

Broccoli & "Cheese" 88

Easiest Corn on the Cob 91

Two-Minute Lemon Asparagus 92

Snappy Soups 95

Cream-Free Zuppa Toscana 96

No-Cans-Needed Chicken &
Wild Rice Soup 99

Potato & Sausage Soup 100

Green Chile Chicken Enchilada Soup 103

Vegan & Gluten-Free Minestrone 104

Ham & No-Soak Bean Soup 107

No-Crust-Needed Pizza Soup 108

No-Red-Meat Chili 111

Ham & Corn Chowder 112

Creamy White Chicken Chili 115

Chicken & Mexican Rice Soup 116

Thai Coconut Soup 119

Cream-Free Tomato Bisque 120

Homemade Bone Broth 123

Chicken & (Rice) Noodle Soup 124

Speedy Sweets 127

Raspberry Orange Rice Pudding 128

Chocolate Pudding Cake 131

Dairy-Free Chocolate Fondue 132

Chocolate Mint Pudding 135

Oat-Free Peach Cobbler 136

Acknowledgments 138

About the Author 140

Index 141

Introduction

Allergists are great at telling you what you can't eat, but they're not dietitians. So, you leave their office with your new diagnosis, not knowing how to cope or cook within your new limitations. It's a scary and isolating feeling, one with which I'm all too familiar. My goal with this book is to save you from that experience. I've spent years developing and testing recipes that cater to the immense amount of food allergies in my family, and now I'm sharing my favorites with you and your family.

Before my college roommate with celiac disease, I'd never met anyone with food allergies or any kind of eating intolerance. Fast-forward to having my first baby. In addition to all of the worry and cautiousness that already goes into raising a human for the first time, we had no idea what other stress was coming. When my son was just a few months old, I started noticing that he would get rashes after nursing. Our pediatrician thought something I was eating was bothering him and had me go on an elimination diet. I remember feeling as though I was starving and had no idea how to think outside of the culinary box in which I had grown up. I had never eaten vegetarian or dairy-free—it was a real shock realizing there was milk made from *rice*! I remember thinking, *Okay, I can do this for six months until he supposedly grows out of his "immature immune system."* Little did I know, I was saying good-bye forever to how I ate.

In his first year, we cut out eggs, soy and wheat. It seems ironic to me that I thought that was so hard, as we now avoid over thirty foods! It's funny and a blessing how "hard" is relative and your capacity grows with time.

The first time my son tried dairy, at eleven months old, is burned into my brain. I fed him Key lime Greek yogurt, thinking I was such a good mom for giving him the "healthier" yogurt. Within minutes, he started acting up. It soon turned into full-blown anaphylaxis—he was vomiting, swollen, red as a lobster and his eyes rolled back. I didn't know what anaphylaxis was, didn't have an EpiPen and didn't think to call 911. I just raced to the ER, screaming his name while I drove to keep him awake. I ran with him in my arms, yelling for help as I rushed through the ER doors. That was when we first realized we were dealing with something more serious than an "immature immune system."

On top of traditional allergies, my son was diagnosed with eosinophilic esophagitis (EOE). He now has eight anaphylactic allergies and has to avoid an additional twenty-plus foods due to his rare disease. I remember the day I found he could no longer eat spinach. I just bawled. Spinach. *Spinach?!* How will he be healthy without this superfood? My son has been a rock through all the testing, surgeries and eating such a limited diet. He is one of my heroes. It truly is an honor to raise him.

It took some more crying and endless hours of scrolling through Pinterest to realize that everything took tweaking. It took wasted ingredients, finding out what we liked and what worked. I knew I would stay in the kitchen all day if that's what it took to discover delicious substitutions so that my son wouldn't go without. I vowed to find a way for all of us to be able to eat the same meal at dinner and to truly enjoy the flavors, rather than just grinning and bearing it.

I'm here to tell you that feeding your allergic family can be done. That you *can* cook to the lowest common denominator and feed your entire family just one meal instead of making multiple variations. And if you're just beginning or you're feeling isolated and discouraged, you are absolutely *not* alone. This hard thing will become your new normal. You will rise above this and you will enjoy food again. If, with this book, I can save you from guesswork and the failed attempts, I want to do that.

With the addition of the Instant Pot® my parents got me several Christmases ago, allergy cooking has become even easier. (Thanks, Mom and Dad!) I love that it cuts down drastically on cooking time. I love that if I forgot to thaw meat, I can still cook it to fork-tender. I love that I can cook soups with dried beans and potatoes that come out buttery soft. And, I love that almost all recipes can be done in the single pot, saving me cleanup.

I hope with the ease of the Instant Pot® plus my allergy-friendly recipes, you can once again look forward to making dinner. You can feel comfortable inviting company over for dinner because you can be proud of your allergy-free dishes. You can stop feeling as though you're stuck in a continual rotation of boring food.

From my allergic family to yours—may your kitchen once again become a happy place. And, may we all keep our children safe and help them be resilient.

Much love,
Megan Lavin & my allergic crew

Things to Note Before You Get Cooking

Ingredients

The American Academy of Allergy, Asthma & Immunology (AAAAI) lists the following eight foods as the most common triggers of food allergies/intolerances:

- Cow's milk
- Eggs
- Fish
- Peanuts
- Shellfish
- Soy
- Tree nuts
- Wheat

The recipes in this book have been developed to avoid these eight allergens. In some instances, alternative ingredients are suggested—such as wheat-free soy sauce or coconut aminos (for soy-free)—to allow the reader to select which of the two is more appropriate.

Please carefully read the ingredients list of commercially prepared products to ensure the item you use is completely free of whatever allergen(s) need to be avoided. For example, some brands of chicken bouillon contain dairy, and commercially made mayonnaise often includes soy.

The AAAAI does not consider coconut a tree nut, and neither do I. So, you will see I use cans of full-fat coconut milk in several recipes. When I list that as an ingredient, I *always* mean to use the stuff from the can you find in the international food aisle. I never use the boxed carton you find in the dairy aisle; that is too watered down. If you have an allergy to coconut, but not other nuts, you can try using cashew milk, as that also has a creamier, thicker texture. If you cannot do either, you can try using rice milk. This is thinner, so you'll want to start with about half of what the recipe calls for, and then work your way up while watching your consistency.

Be sure to always stand back when you do a quick release because the hot steam can burn you, or damage things above it (e.g., cabinets). Be sure everything is clear when you do so. This will take several minutes. Once all of the pressure is gone, the Instant Pot® will allow you to open the lid.

Meat tenderness is affected by how thick a cut of meat is, and obviously what type. If you open your lid and test your meat and find that it's not as tender as you would like, simply close the lid and try additional five-minute increments, and that should do the trick!

ONE

Get a Move On Mains

The diverse array of entrées in this chapter will make this cookbook your dinner bible. The one I wish I had five years ago.

Long before I had kids, I had dreams of my future family sitting at the table together, enjoying the same meal and having that time be sacred—a routine to close our day over delicious food and connecting conversation. As my son's list of allergies grew, I remember wondering whether I would ever be able to make just one entrée for my family ever again. Being the stubborn person that I am, I was not willing to give up on my dream of a family dinner.

These mains are enjoyed by my *entire* family—whether they have zero food allergies or 30. I was sure to have recipe testers with no food restrictions try these to make sure you can proudly serve them to both your allergic family and company, too! And thanks to the Instant Pot®, they come together so quickly—most are done in under 30 minutes—and make cleanup a breeze.

I covered all of the typical mains—you know, the ones you miss the most—including Tomatillo Pork Tacos (page 28) for taco Tuesday, a few meatless Monday options (hello, Quinoa Nachos! [page 27]), and impressive supper options, such as my Classic Sunday Roast (page 55).

If you feel as though your main dishes are in a rut because your diet is so limited, turn the page to find some new top eight—free family favorites.

Turns out, some dreams do come true!

No-Stir Stir-Fry

This is a favorite weeknight meal for its ease as well as flavor. Instead of having to stand over a hot wok and constantly stir your meat and veggies around, you can simply throw them *and* your noodles in the Instant Pot and let it work its magic. It will blow your mind that your chicken and noodles only need to cook for five minutes! Feel free to switch up the veggies to help clean out your fridge and pantry! You can also omit the chicken for a meatless option.

SERVES 4

1 tbsp (15 ml) olive oil

1 lb (455 g) chicken breasts, cut into bite-size pieces

½ cup (120 ml) low-sodium gluten-free soy sauce or coconut aminos

2½ tbsp (38 g) light brown sugar

2 tbsp (30 ml) rice vinegar

½ tsp chili garlic paste (e.g., sriracha)

2 cloves garlic, diced (about 1 tsp)

2 cups (475 ml) water

7 oz (198 g) uncooked rice noodles (I like Thai Kitchen Stir-Fry Rice Noodles)

1 red bell pepper, seeded and sliced thinly (see notes)

8 oz (225 g) baby corn, drained

8 oz (225 g) water chestnuts, drained

⅓ cup (43 g) frozen petite peas, thawed

Green onions and/or sesame seeds, for garnish

Place your olive oil, chicken, soy sauce, brown sugar, rice vinegar, chili garlic paste, garlic, water and rice noodles in your Instant Pot. Close the lid and move the valve to SEALING. Use the PRESSURE button to set your Instant Pot to high pressure. Hit MANUAL and press the plus and minus buttons to reach 5 minutes.

Once the timer is done, move the valve to VENTING to quickly release the pressure. Once you can open the lid, turn off the Instant Pot to kill any heat so that the noodles don't become overcooked.

Add your sliced bell pepper, baby corn, water chestnuts and peas. Stir everything well, being sure to break up any noodles that may have clumped while cooking.

Serve garnished with green onions and/or sesame seeds.

NOTES: If you wish, you can add the bell pepper before closing the lid. We prefer more snap and texture, so we like ours raw, but some may prefer their bell pepper cooked in this type of dish. Also, I use chicken breasts for all my chicken recipes, but chicken thighs would work great here and in any other chicken recipe!

Honey Garlic Chicken & Broccoli

Since we don't dare try takeout with the possible cross-contamination of nuts and wheat, I've learned how to re-create some of our favorite Asian American dishes. This sticky sweet honey glaze coats the broccoli and chicken and makes for the most delightful dinner. Served over rice, it gives you your protein, veggies and carbs in one bowl (and I love one-bowl dinners). I absolutely adore not having to think of an additional side dish!

SERVES 4

2 chicken breasts (about 1 lb [455 g]), cut into bite-size pieces

⅓ cup (115 g) honey

2 tbsp (30 ml) gluten-free soy sauce or coconut aminos

½ to 1 tsp sriracha

4 cloves garlic, minced (about 2 tsp [6 g])

2 medium heads broccoli, cut into florets

⅓ cup (80 ml) cold water

2 tbsp (16 g) cornstarch or arrowroot powder

Cooked rice or quinoa, for serving

Green onions and sesame seeds, for garnish (optional)

Place your chicken, honey, soy sauce, sriracha and garlic in your Instant Pot. Close the lid and move the valve to SEALING. Use the PRESSURE button to set your Instant Pot to high pressure. Hit MANUAL and use the plus and minus buttons to reach 6 minutes.

Once the timer is done, move the valve to VENTING to quickly release the pressure.

Open the lid and place your broccoli florets in the pot. Secure the lid and move the valve to SEALING. Hit MANUAL and use the plus and minus buttons to reach 0 minutes. (Zero minutes will allow it to come to pressure and then turn right off, which I find cooks broccoli perfectly.)

Once the timer is done, move the valve to VENTING to quickly release the pressure.

Using a slotted spoon, remove your chicken and broccoli from the Instant Pot. Hit SAUTÉ to bring the sauce to a boil. In a small bowl, whisk together the cold water and cornstarch. Once the sauce is boiling, add this slurry. Allow your sauce to boil for at least 1 minute, stirring frequently. Once it has reached your desired consistency (the sauce will thicken as it cools), turn off the Instant Pot and add back the chicken and broccoli. Stir well to coat.

Serve over cooked rice or quinoa. Garnish with green onions and sesame seeds, if so desired.

TIP: Since we eat rice a lot, I'll make a huge batch in the Instant Pot to last the week and store it in the fridge. Then, I'll just re-heat how much I need for each dinner.

Sweet & Tangy Pineapple Chicken

Back when my son's only safe protein was chicken I wanted as many variations of it as I could get. We adore pineapple for its tropical, bright flavors and I love sweet sauces, so this was a welcome recipe in the rotation. Even though we now have more meats in our diet, this recipe has stuck around. When I'm serving it to my children, I omit the red pepper flakes, but if your palate likes a touch of heat, I'd recommend it! For smaller eaters, I cook the chicken breasts whole and then shred them before returning the meat to the pot so that it's easier to eat.

SERVES 4

Juice from 1 (20-oz [570-g]) can pineapple slices, pineapple reserved

⅔ cup (150 g) light brown sugar

¼ cup (60 ml) fresh lemon juice

2 tbsp (30 ml) gluten-free soy sauce or coconut aminos

½ tsp ground ginger

½ tsp red pepper flakes (optional)

2 boneless, skinless chicken breasts (about 1 lb [455 g])

2 medium heads broccoli, cut into florets

2 tbsp (16 g) cornstarch or arrowroot powder

⅓ cup (80 ml) cold water

Cooked rice or quinoa, for serving

Sliced green onions, for garnish

In a mixing bowl, stir together your pineapple juice, brown sugar, lemon juice, soy sauce, ginger and red pepper flakes, if using.

Place your chicken breasts in your Instant Pot and pour the pineapple juice mixture over the chicken. Close the lid and move the valve to SEALING. Use the PRESSURE button to set your Instant Pot to high pressure. Hit MANUAL and use the plus and minus buttons to reach 10 minutes.

Once the timer is done, move the valve to VENTING to quickly release the pressure.

Open the lid and add your broccoli florets. Close the lid and move the valve to SEALING. Hit MANUAL and use the plus and minus buttons to reach 0 minutes.

Once the timer is done, move the valve to VENTING to quickly release the pressure.

Open the lid and remove the chicken and broccoli with a slotted spoon. Hit SAUTÉ to bring the sauce to a boil. In a small bowl, whisk together the cornstarch and water. Once the sauce is boiling, add this slurry. Allow your sauce to boil for at least 1 minute, stirring frequently. Once it has reached your desired consistency (the sauce will thicken as it cools), turn off the Instant Pot and add back the chicken and broccoli. Stir well to coat. Serve the chicken, broccoli and sauce over cooked rice or quinoa. Garnish with the reserved pineapple and green onions.

Healthier-for-You Orange Chicken

You once enjoyed the zesty, bright bursts of orange syrup cascading over chicken—and you can once again! This time without wheat breading, egg batter, frying or having to wait in line at a drive-through! In this healthy yet equally tasty version, you'll notice I use only one chicken breast, as I like to have half meat and half cauliflower. This saves on our meat budget and I feel better getting in more veggies. If you're not a cauliflower fan, you can omit the cauliflower and double the chicken.

SERVES 4

1 tsp sesame oil or olive oil

3 tbsp (45 ml) gluten-free soy sauce or coconut aminos

Zest of 1 orange

¾ cup (175 ml) fresh orange juice

½ cup (115 g) light brown sugar

2 tsp (4 g) ground ginger

2 cloves garlic, minced (about 1 tsp)

2 tbsp (30 ml) rice vinegar

¼ tsp red pepper flakes (optional)

1 chicken breast (about 1 lb [455 g]), diced into bite-size pieces (see headnote)

1 small head cauliflower, chopped into small florets

½ cup (120 ml) cold water

2 tbsp (16 g) cornstarch or arrowroot powder

Cooked rice or quinoa, for serving

Green onion, chopped, for garnish

Place your sesame oil, soy sauce, orange zest and juice, brown sugar, ginger, garlic, vinegar and pepper flakes, if using, in your Instant Pot. Stir well to incorporate everything.

Next, add your diced chicken. Close the lid. Use the PRESSURE button to set your Instant Pot to high pressure. Hit MANUAL and use the plus and minus buttons to reach 6 minutes.

Once the timer is done, move the valve to VENTING to quickly release the pressure.

Open the lid and add the cauliflower florets. Close the lid, move the valve to seal and hit MANUAL. Press the plus or minus buttons to reach 1 minute.

Once the timer is done, move the valve to VENTING to quickly release the pressure. Open the lid and use a slotted spoon to remove the chicken and cauliflower.

Hit SAUTÉ to bring the sauce to a boil. In a small bowl, whisk together the cold water and cornstarch. Once the sauce is boiling, add the slurry. Allow your sauce to boil for at least 1 minute, stirring frequently. Once it has reached your desired consistency (the sauce will thicken as it cools), turn off the Instant Pot and add back the chicken and cauliflower. Stir well to coat.

Serve the chicken, cauliflower and sauce over cooked rice or quinoa and garnish with green onions.

No-Butter Indian "Butter" Chicken

Don't let the name fool you—there's no butter or dairy here, just loads of spices. While it's not traditional to have carrots in the recipe, I love to sneak in extra veggies for my kids, and it's easier and tastier to have the protein and side all blanketed in the same flavorful sauce. I started with frozen chicken breasts because, if you're like me, you often forget to set them out to thaw ahead of time! If your chicken is not frozen, you can reduce the initial cooking time by half.

SERVES 4

2 frozen chicken breasts (about 1 lb [455 g])

1 tsp salt

⅛ tsp cayenne pepper, or more to heat preference

½ tsp ground ginger

½ tsp ground turmeric

½ tsp ground paprika

½ tsp ground cumin

1 tsp garam masala, divided

1 cup (180 g) canned diced tomatoes, undrained

2 medium carrots, peeled and finely diced

3 cloves garlic, minced (about 1½ tsp [5 g])

¼ cup (60 ml) coconut oil

¼ cup (60 ml) canned full-fat coconut milk

Cooked rice or quinoa, for serving

Fresh cilantro, chopped, for garnish (optional)

Place your frozen chicken breasts, salt, cayenne, ginger, turmeric, paprika, cumin and ½ teaspoon of the garam masala in your Instant Pot and place the diced tomatoes on top. Use the PRESSURE button to set your Instant Pot to high pressure. Close the lid, and move the valve to SEALING. Hit MANUAL and use the plus and minus buttons to reach 23 minutes.

Once the timer is done, move the valve to VENTING to quickly release the pressure.

Open the lid and add the diced carrots. Close the lid, move the valve to SEALING and hit MANUAL; then use the plus and minus buttons to reach 1 minute.

Once the timer is done, move the valve to VENTING to quickly release the pressure and open the lid once it's safe to do so. Take out the chicken and shred it. Return it to the pot once it's shredded.

Add the remaining ½ teaspoon of garam masala and the garlic, coconut oil and coconut milk to the Instant Pot and stir to combine.

Serve over cooked rice or quinoa and garnish with cilantro, if desired.

Sweet Barbacoa

This recipe is adapted from a family favorite that used to take eight hours to marinate and eight hours to cook in a slower cooker. Now, there's no need to marinate and the cooking time is done in only one hour, although the meat tastes as if it cooked all day! The trick is to leave the fat on the roast while it cooks and to cut the meat into four to five pieces. This helps ensure that the sauce can reach more surface area and helps the pressure cooker tenderize it faster. The Dr Pepper adds a hint of sweetness to this juicy cut. Great for bowls or stuffed in a burrito with my Cilantro, Garlic & Lime Rice & Beans (page 64), this is one meat we love to eat for leftovers again and again. If you want it to be extra filling, I like to add a can of drained and rinsed black beans once it's been shredded. For all my recipes that use pork roasts, I find that a fattier and darker cut, such as a Boston butt, works best.

SERVES 4 TO 6

1 (2- to 3-lb [905-g to 1.4-kg]) pork shoulder roast

Salt and pepper

1 (8-oz [235-ml]) can Dr Pepper

8 oz (225 g) tomato sauce

1 (8-oz [225-g]) can diced green chiles, undrained (I like mild)

½ tsp garlic powder

½ tsp ground cumin

1 tsp chili powder

½ cup (115 g) light brown sugar

Cut your pork roast into at least 4 pieces. Generously salt and pepper the meat. Lay the pieces in your Instant Pot.

Pour the Dr Pepper, tomato sauce, green chiles, garlic powder, cumin, chili powder and brown sugar on top of the roast. Close the lid and move the valve to SEALING. Use the PRESSURE button to set your Instant Pot to high pressure. Hit MANUAL and use the plus and minus buttons to reach 55 minutes.

Once the timer is done, move the valve to VENTING to quickly release the pressure. If you like your sauce thicker, after you've opened the lid and removed the meat, press SAUTÉ to let it boil and reduce for several minutes.

Transfer the roast to a cutting board and trim off and discard any excess fat. Shred the roast and add it back to the sauce.

Serve the roast over cooked rice, in a salad or in burritos. Best if served with my Cilantro, Garlic & Lime Rice & Beans (page 64).

Chili Lime Chicken Tacos

One of my favorite recipes of the entire cookbook! My recipe tester's only complaint was that she wished she would have doubled the recipe because it was that good. The punch from the limes and the flavor from the salsa verde make this a taco night to remember! Besides the ease of store-bought salsa verde, I also created this recipe with frozen chicken breasts in mind to really help for that busy weeknight meal.

SERVES 4

2 tbsp (30 ml) olive oil

4 frozen chicken breasts (about 2 lb [905 g])

⅓ cup (86 g) salsa verde

2 tsp (5 g) chili powder

1 tsp ground cumin

1 tsp onion powder

1 tsp salt

Zest of 2 limes

Juice of 2 limes (about ¼ cup [60 ml])

4 cloves garlic, minced (about 2 tsp [6 g])

Warmed corn tortillas, for serving

OPTIONAL TOPPINGS

Cooked rice

Thick & Creamy Refried Beans (page 84)

Guacamole

Tomatoes

Fresh cilantro

Chopped lettuce

Pico de gallo

Place your olive oil, chicken, salsa verde, chili powder, cumin, onion powder, salt and lime zest in your Instant Pot. Close the lid and push the valve to SEALING. Use the PRESSURE button to set your Instant Pot to high pressure. Hit MANUAL and use the plus and minus buttons to reach 25 minutes.

After the timer is done, move the valve to VENTING to quickly release the pressure.

Open the lid and shred the chicken. Stir in the lime juice and garlic.

Serve on warmed corn tortillas with your choice of toppings. Don't forget the guac!

NOTE: You'll notice in some recipe directions that I frequently add the garlic *after* the other ingredients are done cooking, so that it's not muted and fresher, because it should be strong in that recipe. If you'd rather put it in all at once, it just won't be as strong but won't ruin the recipe.

Quinoa Nachos

We are big quinoa lovers around here, and we also love Mexican food, so this pairing is *the* best combo. You won't even miss ground beef with this well-seasoned meatless topping. If you need this to be fully vegan, be sure you use vegan bouillon. I love the casualness of this dish, as I simply bring the pan to the table and we all lean in and go to town, picking out the chips that are filled to the brim with toppings. It's hard to not fight for the pieces with the extra avocado! If it's difficult for you to find dairy-free sour cream or cheese, these don't make or break the recipe. We often do it without either of these because the topping is so flavorful.

SERVES 4

1 tbsp (15 ml) olive oil

2 cloves garlic, finely minced (about 1 tsp)

⅓ poblano chile, seeded and finely diced (about ⅓ to ½ cup [48 to 72 g])

1 cup (173 g) uncooked quinoa, well rinsed and drained

1¼ cups (285 ml) low-sodium chicken broth (or 1¼ cups [285 ml] water + 2 tsp [4 g] chicken or vegan bouillon powder)

8 oz (235 g) tomato sauce

1 (15-oz [425-g]) can black beans, drained and rinsed

1 tsp salt

1 tsp chili powder

½ tsp dried oregano

1 tsp ground cumin

1 to 2 tbsp (15 to 30 ml) fresh lime juice, according to taste

½ cup (20 g) chopped fresh cilantro

6 oz (170 g) tortilla chips (about ½ large bag)

4 oz (115 g) dairy-free cheese shreds

OPTIONAL TOPPINGS

Fresh cilantro

Jalapeño

Salsa

Dairy-free sour cream

Guacamole or avocado slices

Olives

Fresh tomato, diced

Place your olive oil, garlic, poblano, quinoa, broth, tomato sauce, black beans, salt, chili powder, oregano and cumin in your Instant Pot. Use the PRESSURE button to set your Instant Pot to high pressure. Close the lid and move the valve to SEALING. Hit MANUAL and use the plus and minus buttons to reach 1 minute.

Once the timer shows "L:10" (meaning the pot has cooked for the 1 minute and has also been on LOW or WARM for an additional 10 minutes), go ahead and quickly release any leftover pressure so you can open the lid. Pour in your lime juice and top with the cilantro.

Spread an even layer of tortilla chips on a sheet pan. Using a spoon, dollop the quinoa mixture evenly all over the chips (much like you'd do with ground taco meat). Sprinkle your dairy-free cheese on top. If desired, throw the sheet pan in the oven and set to BROIL to melt the cheese further for 1 to 2 minutes.

After broiling, sprinkle the nachos with your desired toppings.

Save any additional quinoa mixture in an airtight container for 2 to 3 days. Keep the chips and the quinoa mixture stored separately.

Tomatillo Pork Tacos

A street taco at its finest. The pork in this recipe cooks in a blended batch of garlic, tomatillos and cilantro for an easy yet fresh sauce. My kids lovingly call these "green tacos," thanks to all the green veggies that tint the sauce. Fork-tender pork with a bright note from the finishing touches of lime—I can hardly warm tortillas fast enough to keep up with my kids' quick inhalation of them.

SERVES 4

1 tsp salt, plus more to taste for seasoning

Pepper, for seasoning

1 (2- to 3-lb [905-g to 1.4-kg]) pork roast

2 tbsp (30 ml) olive oil

½ lb (335 g) tomatillos, husked and quartered

1 red onion, roughly chopped

½ jalapeño pepper, seeded

6 cloves garlic, minced (about 1 tbsp [10 g])

½ cup (120 ml) chicken broth (or ½ cup [120 ml] water + 1 tsp chicken bouillon powder)

½ cup (20 g) fresh cilantro

3 tbsp (45 ml) fresh lime juice

For Serving

Warmed corn tortillas

Guacamole

Thick & Creamy Refried Beans (page 84)

Fresh cilantro

Salt and pepper your pork roast generously on both sides. Cut the roast into 6 equal pieces. Place the pork in your Instant Pot.

In a high-quality blender or food processor, combine your olive oil, tomatillos, red onion, jalapeño, garlic, broth, salt and the cilantro. Blend until everything is smooth. Pour the blended sauce onto the meat.

Close the lid and move the valve to SEALING. Use the PRESSURE button to set your Instant Pot to high pressure. Hit MANUAL and hit the plus and minus buttons to reach 60 minutes.

When the timer is done, remove the meat from the pot. Carve off the fat and discard it. Shred the rest of the meat.

Before returning the meat to the pot, remove all but I cup (235 ml) of the remaining juices. Stir the meat and the remaining cup of juices together. Add the lime juice. Taste, and adjust the salt and pepper to your liking.

Serve the meat and a little juice in the middle of a warm corn tortilla topped with your favorite toppings.

> NOTE: You'll notice that I always mention chicken bouillon. I prefer to use Orrington Farms Broth Base & Seasonings, which comes in a vegan version as well. I like to use this for the consistency, as well as the fact that I use broth a lot and I hate to keep all of those cartons of liquid. Plus, many liquid and bouillon bases have wheat and dairy in them.

No-Cheese-Needed Ragu

Pre-allergies, we used to buy bottled sauce for ragu and had to put a small mountain of cheese on top to make it satisfactory. Since coming up with this thick, hearty and perfectly seasoned ragu, I find I don't miss my cheese shavings anymore! The notion that all Italian food needs to be slathered in cheese is false! Enjoy this classic, made dairy-free, and say good-bye to the bottled stuff. Also—this makes enough that we always have leftovers for lunch, or I freeze the extra sauce by itself to save for a crazy night so all I have to do is boil noodles. It's my go-to on busy nights. And, if you want it to be vegetarian, simply omit the sausage, as the mushrooms create plenty of texture on their own.

SERVES 4

1 tbsp (15 ml) extra virgin olive oil

1 large red onion, diced finely

1 lb (455 g) Italian sausage

1 (6-oz [170-g]) can tomato paste

1 (28-oz [800-g]) can basil, garlic and oregano diced tomatoes

8 oz (225 g) mushrooms, sliced

1 tsp dried oregano

2 tsp (2 g) dried basil

½ tsp dried thyme

1 bay leaf

4 large cloves garlic, chopped (about 2½ tsp [7 g])

1 tbsp (15 ml) balsamic vinegar

12 oz (340 g) gluten-free spaghetti

Sea salt and pepper, to taste

Splash of honey or agave nectar (optional)

Fresh parsley or basil, for garnish (optional)

Place your olive oil, onion and sausage in your Instant Pot and hit SAUTÉ. Cook until the onion is soft and the meat is browned, 3 to 5 minutes, stirring often. Turn off the SAUTÉ function.

Add your tomato paste, diced tomatoes, mushrooms, oregano, basil, thyme, bay leaf, garlic and balsamic vinegar. Close the lid. Use the PRESSURE button to set your Instant Pot to high pressure. Move the valve to SEALING. Hit MANUAL and use the plus and minus buttons to reach 10 minutes.

Meanwhile, boil your spaghetti according to package directions until al dente. Drain, rinse and set aside.

Once the sauce is done, move the valve to VENTING to quickly release the pressure. Open the lid and stir. Taste and adjust the salt and pepper. If it's too acidic, add a splash of honey or agave. Discard the bay leaf.

Place the spaghetti on a plate and ladle the sauce over the top. Garnish with fresh parsley or basil, if so desired. If there are any leftovers, store the noodles and sauce separately.

TIP: Because gluten-free noodles have so much starch, they can be gummy. To avoid this, I run my noodles under cold water after they've cooked to rinse off the excess starch.

Bread Crumb– & Egg-Free Italian Meatballs & Spaghetti

I often feel as though heaven must be guiding me as I just go for it and try something crazy in the kitchen. I knew I wanted a meatball recipe for this cookbook but had never successfully made an Italian version (I have a teriyaki and an Asian version on my website). Plus—I'd never made them in the Instant Pot. I prayed the quinoa would hold as the binder, shut the lid and crossed my fingers *and* toes. Angels must have whispered this recipe in my ears, because it keeps its shape, has great texture and tastes, pun intended, *amaze-balls*. My kids are still asking when we can have these again.

SERVES 4

⅔ cup (160 ml) water

⅓ cup (58 g) uncooked quinoa

2 cloves garlic, finely minced (about 1 tsp)

1½ tsp (1.5 g) dried oregano

1½ tsp (1 g) granulated onion powder

1 tsp dried basil

½ tsp dried parsley

½ tsp salt

1 lb (455 g) Italian sausage

1 (24-oz [710-ml]) bottle tomato basil marinara sauce

1 (12-oz [340-g]) package gluten-free spaghetti

Fresh basil or parsley, for garnish (optional)

Place your water and quinoa in your Instant Pot. Close the lid. Use the PRESSURE button to set your Instant Pot to high pressure. Move the valve to SEALING. Hit MANUAL and use the plus and minus buttons to reach 1 minute.

Once the timer is done, allow the pot to sit for 10 minutes. Once the display shows "L:10," move the valve to VENTING to finish releasing any leftover pressure.

Once the quinoa is cool enough to handle, place it in a bowl with the garlic, oregano, onion powder, basil, parsley, salt and Italian sausage. Mix well by hand.

Form the meatballs by hand, making them about 2 inches (5 cm) in diameter. Pour half of the bottle of marinara sauce into the bottom in the Instant Pot. Place the meatballs on top of the sauce and pour the rest of the sauce on top.

Close the lid and move the valve to SEALING. Hit MANUAL and use the plus and minus buttons to reach 10 minutes.

While the meatballs cook, boil your spaghetti according to package directions until al dente; then drain and rinse.

Once the timer is done, move the valve to VENTING to quickly release the steam.

Serve the meatballs and sauce over your pasta and garnish with fresh basil or parsley, if so desired.

> NOTE: I used to use brown rice noodles for pasta dishes, but found that those don't hold up in hot soups or the next day in leftovers. The brands that have both rice and corn have a much better texture.

Tuscan White Bean Quinoa Salad

As mentioned earlier, we *love* quinoa around these parts. And I love Mediterranean flavors. And, if there can be a refrigerated salad that only continues to marinate and gets better in time, I am in heaven. This salad exceeds all those criteria! Meatless, filled with veggies and dripping in a delicious balsamic dressing, this is perfect for a light dinner, or it can even be doubled and brought as a side to a potluck. I crave a good bite from red onion, but if you want your onion less potent, add it to the quinoa before you cook, instead of adding it raw afterward. Also, you can play with the amounts of beans, olives and vegetables to your liking—this salad is very forgiving.

SERVES 4

SALAD

1 cup (173 g) uncooked quinoa

1½ cups (355 ml) water

1 tbsp (6 g) chicken bouillon powder

½ (15-oz [425-g]) can white beans, drained and rinsed

½ (15-oz [425-g]) can black olives, drained and halved

½ cucumber, diced (about ⅓ cup [40 g])

½ cup (75 g) cherry tomatoes, halved

½ red bell pepper, seeded and diced (about ⅓ cup [50 g])

¼ cup (40 g) finely diced red onion

2 tbsp (5 g) fresh basil, chopped finely

DRESSING

¼ cup (60 ml) balsamic vinegar

¼ cup (60 ml) olive oil

2 cloves garlic, minced finely (about 1 tsp)

2 tsp (8 g) sugar

½ tsp dried oregano

¼ tsp salt

¼ tsp freshly ground black pepper

To prepare the salad, place your quinoa, water and bouillon in your Instant Pot. Close the lid and move the valve to SEALING. Use the PRESSURE button to set your Instant Pot to high pressure. Hit MANUAL and use the plus and minus buttons to reach 1 minute.

Once the timer is done, leave the lid on and allow it to sit for 10 minutes.

Meanwhile, make the dressing. In a jar with a sealable lid, combine your balsamic vinegar, olive oil, garlic, sugar, oregano, salt and pepper. Close the lid and shake well to mix.

Once the timer on the Instant Pot reads "L:10," move the valve to VENTING to finish releasing any leftover pressure. Turn off the Instant Pot. Open the lid.

Stir the quinoa and add your beans, olives, cucumber, tomatoes, bell pepper, onion and basil. If serving immediately, top with the dressing to your desired taste (it's best to start with a small amount and work your way up). This can be served warm or cold; I prefer cold.

Creamy Italian Chicken & Pasta

Ever since going dairy-free, I've lamented over missing a creamy, dreamy, comforting pasta dish. This is *the* creamiest I've ever made, and I truly didn't know I would ever experience this texture again. Rice noodles are slathered in thick sauce, making them absolutely slurpable. This is now one of my husband's favorite pasta dishes (and that's saying something—his adoptive mom was an Italian woman in Boston!). The only wheat- and dairy-free Italian dressing mix I have found is by Simply Organic, but feel free to use whatever one works for your allergies.

SERVES 4

1 tbsp (15 ml) olive oil

2 chicken breasts, cut into bite-size pieces

1 cup (235 ml) chicken broth (or 1 cup [235 ml] water + 2 tsp [4 g] chicken bouillon powder)

½ cup (120 ml) rice milk

3 cloves garlic, minced (about 1½ tsp [5 g])

½ yellow onion, diced

2 tbsp Italian dressing seasoning mix (about a 0.7-oz [19.5-g] packet)

1 (8-oz [225-g]) package rice noodles (I like Thai Kitchen's Stir-Fry Rice Noodles)

8 oz (225 g) mushrooms, sliced

½ tsp salt, or more to taste

¼ tsp pepper, or more to taste

1 cup (130 g) frozen sweet peas, thawed

4 oz (115 g) dairy-free cream cheese

3 oz (85 g) dairy-free sour cream or additional dairy-free cream cheese

Place the olive oil, chicken, broth, rice milk, garlic, onion, Italian dressing seasoning, noodles, mushrooms, salt and pepper in your Instant Pot. Close the lid and move the valve to SEALING. Use the PRESSURE button to set your Instant Pot to high pressure. Press the MANUAL button and use the plus and minus buttons to reach 6 minutes.

After the timer is done, immediately move the valve to VENTING to quickly release the pressure.

Open the lid and stir in the peas, cream cheese and sour cream, separating the noodles as needed. Taste and adjust the salt and pepper as desired.

The leftovers may thicken, so thin out the sauce as needed with additional rice milk after rewarming.

NOTE: The only dairy-free sour cream I've ever found has soy, so if you can't do that, you can use additional dairy-free cream cheese.

Greek Lemon Chicken & Potatoes

My kids are potato obsessed—I blame my Idaho heritage. And we are suckers for lemon chicken. I combined the two with some classic Greek herbs to make a chicken dish even my middle child, who is quick to proclaim things as "yucky," will eat leftovers of! If you're in a hurry, you can just eat the potatoes soft (still fab!), or if you have the time, you can fry them up for a golden finish (as in the photo). By cooking them first in the Instant Pot, they are able to crisp up extremely well—which is the trick to expertly fried potatoes!

SERVES 4

4 to 5 large potatoes

2 large chicken breasts

1 tbsp (15 ml) olive oil

¼ cup (60 ml) water

2 tsp (4 g) chicken bouillon powder

¼ cup (60 ml) fresh lemon juice, plus more for serving (optional)

1 tsp salt, or more to taste

1½ tsp (1.5 g) dried thyme

1½ tsp (2 g) dried rosemary

2 cloves garlic, minced

Freshly ground black pepper

Canola or grapeseed oil, for frying (optional)

Chopped fresh chives, for garnish (optional)

Peel and dice your potatoes into bite-size pieces. Dice your chicken into pieces the same size as the potatoes.

Place the olive oil in your Instant Pot. Place the diced chicken, potatoes, water, bouillon, lemon juice, salt, thyme, rosemary and garlic on top. Close the lid and move the valve to SEALING. Use the PRESSURE button to set your Instant Pot to high pressure. Press the MANUAL button and use the plus and minus buttons to reach 7 minutes.

Once the timer is done, move the valve to VENTING and release the pressure. Once you're able to open the lid, remove the chicken and potatoes. Shred the chicken.

Taste and adjust the salt and garnish with freshly ground black pepper before serving.

Or, if you'd like crispy potatoes (as in the picture), place enough canola oil to cover a cast-iron skillet to about a ½-inch (1.3-cm) depth. Heat over medium-high and add your potatoes. They should sizzle when you add them. Do not crowd the pan. Allow the potatoes to cook, undisturbed, for 2 to 3 minutes, or until they are golden brown. Flip them and repeat the process, until they are crispy and as golden brown as you like them.

Once the potatoes are done, transfer them to a paper towel to absorb any excess oil, then plate them and top with the chives and a squeeze of fresh lemon juice. Serve next to the shredded chicken.

No-Soak Red Beans & Rice

Even though I plan out my meals and am very organized, I *never* remember to soak my beans the night before. Which stinks, because from-scratch beans are *so* much more flavorful than canned beans, and I love using up all the dried beans I have in my food storage. I was relieved to find out that the Instant Pot can take dried beans to cooked beans in less than an hour! Add some Creole spices and sausage and you have a seriously delicious dinner. And best of all, this is flexible! If you can't have Worcestershire sauce because of the fish and soy in it, you can omit it, as well as the sausages if you want it to be vegetarian.

SERVES 4

2 tbsp (30 ml) olive oil

1 large red onion, diced small

2½ tsp (3 g) dried thyme

2½ tsp (3 g) dried oregano

2 tsp (12 g) salt, or more to taste

1 lb (455 g) dried red kidney beans, rinsed

4 cups (945 ml) chicken broth (or 4 cups [945 ml] water + 8 tsp [16 g] chicken bouillon powder)

3 tbsp (45 ml) gluten-free Worcestershire sauce

1 tsp Tabasco sauce or your favorite brand of hot sauce, or to taste

3 bay leaves

2½ tsp (12 ml) red wine vinegar

1 cup (225 g) diced Cajun spiced chicken sausages (2 to 3 sausages), cut into bite-size pieces

7 to 8 cloves garlic, minced (2½ tbsp [25 g])

Freshly ground black pepper, to taste

Cooked rice, for serving

Turn your Instant Pot to the SAUTÉ function. Add the olive oil, and once hot, add the onion. Cook, stirring frequently, until the onion is softened, 2 to 4 minutes.

Turn off the Instant Pot and add the thyme, oregano, salt, beans, broth, Worcestershire, Tabasco, bay leaves, vinegar and sausages.

Stir; then close the lid of the pot. Use the PRESSURE button to set your Instant Pot to high pressure and turn the valve to SEALING. Hit MANUAL and use the plus and minus buttons to reach 60 minutes.

After the timer is done, naturally release the pressure.

Open the lid and pick out any shriveled beans that have floated to the top. Add the garlic. Taste and adjust the salt as needed, and add pepper to taste. Discard the bay leaves.

Place the cooked rice in a bowl and spoon the beans and the glorious sauce over the rice.

Store any leftover rice and beans separately. This keeps for 3 days refrigerated in an airtight container; it also freezes well.

Shellfish-Free Jambalaya

Although jambalaya is typically filled with shrimp, this version is still loaded with spices, beans and rice but not the shellfish. Colorful and loaded with veggies, this is a hearty meal that I feel good about giving my kids! In fact, it's so hearty you can omit the sausages to make it vegetarian, if you would like. By using canned beans, this only needs to cook for five minutes, making it great for busy weeknights. This recipe makes a big batch, so you can also enjoy it for lunch the next day, too. Feel free to use any color of bell peppers you like; I'm just a color junkie!

SERVES 4

¼ cup (60 ml) olive oil

1 red onion, diced

2 celery ribs, cut into half-moons

2 medium carrots, cut into half-moons

½ red bell pepper, seeded and diced

½ yellow bell pepper, seeded and diced

½ orange bell pepper, seeded and diced

4 cloves garlic, minced (about 2 tsp [6 g])

4 oz (115 g) mushrooms, sliced

2 bay leaves

2 tsp (2 g) dried oregano

1¾ tsp (11 g) salt, or more to taste

1 tsp paprika

1 tsp dried parsley

½ tsp dried thyme

Pinch of cayenne pepper (or more if you like the heat!)

1 (15-oz [425-g]) can diced fire-roasted tomatoes, undrained

1½ cups (293 g) uncooked white rice

1½ cups (355 ml) chicken broth
(or 1½ cups [355 ml] water + 1 tbsp [6 g] chicken bouillon powder)

2 Cajun sausages, cut into half-moons

1 (15-oz [425-g]) can black-eyed peas, drained and rinsed

OPTIONAL

Hot sauce

Fresh parsley, chopped

Freshly ground black pepper

Place your olive oil, onion, celery, carrots, bell peppers, garlic, mushrooms, bay leaves, oregano, salt, paprika, parsley, thyme, cayenne, tomatoes, rice, broth, sausages and black-eyed peas in your Instant Pot. Close the lid and move the valve to SEALING. Use the PRESSURE button to set your Instant Pot to high pressure. Hit MANUAL and use the plus and minus buttons to reach 5 minutes.

Once the timer is done, allow the pressure to release naturally for 5 minutes. Once the timer shows "L:05," move the valve to VENTING to finish releasing any leftover pressure.

Stir well. Taste and adjust the salt. Top with your preferred garnishes, if desired.

Leftovers keep well in the refrigerator for 2 to 3 days in an airtight container.

Creamy Rice-Milk Cajun Chicken Pasta

Thanks to rice milk and dairy-free cream cheese, I've been able to re-create a restaurant favorite I often ordered in the past. Spicy yet saucy, this pasta is bursting with veggies and Creole flavoring. The textures and flavors of soft strands of pasta, the thick sauce, the bite of sausage and vegetables make this not only a feast for the eyes with its color, but a party in the mouth! I have found two types of dairy-free cream cheese—one made of soy and the other made of coconut. Either should work fine!

SERVES 4

1 tbsp (15 ml) olive oil

1½ cups (355 ml) rice milk

1 yellow onion, cut into thin half-moons

1 tsp chicken bouillon powder

2 frozen chicken breasts

1 (12-oz [340-g]) package gluten-free noodles of choice

1 red bell pepper, seeded and sliced

1 orange bell pepper, seeded and sliced

8 oz (225 g) mushrooms, sliced

2 Cajun chicken sausages, cut into half-moons

1½ tsp (9 g) salt, or more to taste

1¼ tsp (3 g) paprika

¼ tsp freshly ground black pepper, or more to taste

½ tsp onion powder

⅛ tsp cayenne pepper (or more if you want to up the heat)

½ tsp dried oregano

¼ tsp dried thyme

3 cloves garlic, minced (about 1½ tsp [5 g])

2 oz (55 g) dairy-free cream cheese, softened

1½ tbsp (12 g) cornstarch or arrowroot powder

1½ tbsp (23 ml) cold water

Fresh parsley, chopped (optional)

Place your olive oil, rice milk, onion, bouillon and frozen chicken breasts in your Instant Pot. Close the lid. Move the valve to SEALING. Use the PRESSURE button to set your Instant Pot to high pressure. Hit MANUAL and use the plus and minus buttons to reach 23 minutes.

Meanwhile, cook your noodles according to the package directions until al dente. Drain, rinse and set aside.

When the timer is done, move the valve to VENTING to quickly release the pressure. Open the lid and add your bell peppers, mushrooms and chicken sausages. Close the lid and move the valve to SEALING. Hit MANUAL and use the plus and minus buttons to reach 2 minutes.

Once the timer is done, move the valve to VENTING to quickly release the pressure.

Remove the chicken from the pot and shred it.

Add your salt, paprika, pepper, onion powder, cayenne, oregano, thyme, garlic and dairy-free cream cheese to the Instant Pot. Stir well to mix them thoroughly until the cream cheese is melted and incorporated.

Press the SAUTÉ button and bring the mixture to a boil. In a small bowl, whisk together the cornstarch and water. Once the sauce is boiling, add the slurry. Allow your sauce to boil for at least 1 minute, stirring frequently. Once it has reached your desired consistency (the sauce will thicken as it cools), turn off the Instant Pot and add back the chicken. Add the cooked pasta. Stir to coat and serve immediately, adjusting salt and pepper to your liking. Garnish with fresh parsley, if desired.

Dripping Balsamic Pork Roast

If you are a balsamic lover, then this recipe is just for you! Rich in color and flavor from the balsamic, this roast is anything but bland. Serve the roast and its drippings over my Dairy-Free Garlic Parsley Mashed Potatoes (page 71), and you have a Sunday dinner dream come true. Since I already have my beaters out for the mashed potatoes, when the roast is done cooking, I'll put them in the Instant Pot, without even rinsing them, for the easiest meat shredding you've ever seen! As always, remember you can omit the Worcestershire if it doesn't match your food allergies. And, if you can stand waiting to cut the fat off the roast until after it's done cooking, I find it comes off easier—plus the fat imparts more flavor while the pork cooks.

SERVES 4

1 (2- to 3-lb [905-g to 1.4-kg]) boneless pork roast

Kosher salt and pepper

1 tsp garlic powder

½ tsp red pepper flakes

⅓ cup (80 ml) chicken broth (or ⅓ cup [80 ml] water + 1 tsp chicken bouillon powder)

⅔ cup (160 ml) balsamic vinegar

2 tbsp (30 ml) gluten-free Worcestershire sauce

2 tbsp (40 g) honey

Dairy-Free Garlic Parsley Mashed Potatoes (page 71), for serving

Cut your pork roast into four equal sections. Salt and pepper the pieces well.

Place the pork in your Instant Pot and top with the garlic powder, pepper flakes, broth, balsamic vinegar, Worcestershire and honey. Close the lid. Move the valve to SEALING. Use the PRESSURE button to set your Instant Pot to high pressure. Hit MANUAL and use the plus and minus buttons to reach 60 minutes.

Once the timer is done, move the valve to VENTING to quickly release the pressure.

Remove and shred the meat. Reserve remaining juices for sauce.

Serve the meat and a generous helping of the delicious sauce over the mashed potatoes.

35-Minute Herb Crusted Turkey Breast

Don't be a turkey and have this beautiful beast only at Thanksgiving time. Once you see how easy it is (and how you don't have to wake up at the crack of dawn to start cooking it), you will want to make turkey for Sunday dinners All. The. Time. You'll never make a turkey in the oven again! Be sure to plan ahead, though, to make sure your turkey breast is completely thawed—this can take several days. And make sure you're getting a turkey breast and not a turkey roast. Lastly, keep in mind the size of your Instant Pot when buying your bird to make sure it will fit!

SERVES 4

TURKEY

1 (4- to 5-lb [1.8- to 2.3-kg]) bone-in turkey breast, completely thawed

1 cup (237 ml) chicken broth (or 1 cup [237 ml] water + 2 tsp [9 g] chicken bouillon powder)

3 tbsp (45 ml) olive oil

2 bay leaves

1 (1-lb [455-g]) package baby carrots

2 yellow onions, chopped roughly

8 oz (225 g) mushrooms, sliced

SEASONINGS

1 tbsp (9 g) dried minced garlic

1 tsp seasoned salt

½ tsp sal, or more to taste

½ tsp freshly ground black pepper, or more to taste

1 tsp Italian seasoning

½ tsp dried parsley

½ tsp dried sage

½ tsp dried thyme

⅓ cup (80 ml) cold water

3 tbsp (24 g) cornstarch or arrowroot powder

Dairy-Free Garlic Parsley Mashed Potatoes (page 71), for serving

Once your turkey is thawed, take it out of its packaging and discard any netting or gravy packets. Remove and discard the skin. This is important, as the skin will not crisp in an Instant Pot as it does in the dry heat of an oven. Plus, the spices will sit on the skin, instead of penetrating the meat.

Place the turkey breast and broth in your Instant Pot. Pour the olive oil over the meat. Tuck in the bay leaves toward the bottom of the pot. Next, tuck the carrots, onions and mushrooms around the meat as best you can, making sure you can still close your Instant Pot. Depending on the size of your turkey, you may not be able to use all of the vegetables, and that is okay.

In a small bowl, combine the garlic, seasoned salt, salt, pepper, Italian seasoning, parsley, sage and thyme. Sprinkle the mixture evenly over the turkey. Close the lid and move the valve to SEALING. Use the PRESSURE button to set your Instant Pot to high pressure. Hit MANUAL and use the plus and minus buttons to reach 35 minutes.

When the timer is done, move the valve to VENTING to quickly release the pressure. Use a meat thermometer to make sure that the turkey registers at least 165°F (74°C). Do not rely on any turkey timers that may be in the turkey. If it is not done, close the lid and continue to cook in 5-minute increments.

Once the turkey is done, carefully lift it out of the pot and allow it to rest. Take out the carrots and set aside on a serving platter. Discard the bay leaves. Blend the remaining juices, onions and mushrooms in a blender (this may take several batches). Add blended juices back to the Instant Pot. Hit SAUTÉ to bring the gravy to a boil. In a small bowl, whisk together the cold water and cornstarch. Once the gravy is boiling, add this slurry. Sauté until your gravy reaches your desired thickness, for 5 to 7 minutes. Taste and adjust the salt and pepper.

Slice the turkey and serve with mashed potatoes, pouring the gravy generously over the turkey and mashed potatoes.

Apricot-Glazed Pork Chops

Apricots do not get used often enough. They're sweet, but not too sweet, and they're the perfect accompaniment to pork chops to help jazz them up in all the right ways. (Hello, date night in!) With a thick and gorgeous glaze, these sit beautifully next to my Lemon Herbed Quinoa (page 67). No need to sear as you normally would, as the Instant Pot imparts the tenderness and flavor all on its own!

SERVES 4

1 tbsp (15 ml) olive oil

4 boneless pork chops (no thicker than ½" [1.3-cm] thick)

1½ tsp (9.5 g) kosher salt

1 tsp garlic powder

1 tsp onion powder

½ tsp freshly ground black pepper

1 tsp ground ginger

½ cup (120 ml) chicken broth (or ½ cup [120 ml] water + 1 tsp chicken bouillon powder)

⅔ cup (213 g) apricot preserves (see note)

Lemon Herbed Quinoa (page 67), for serving

Add the olive oil to your Instant Pot; then lay your pork chops down on top.

In a small bowl, whisk together the salt, garlic powder, onion powder, pepper, ginger, broth and apricot preserves. Pour the mixture over the pork chops.

Close the lid and move the valve to SEALING. Use the PRESSURE button to set your Instant Pot to high pressure. Hit the MANUAL button and use the plus and minus buttons to reach 10 minutes.

Once the timer is done, move the valve to VENTING to quickly release the pressure. Use a meat thermometer to test the temperature of the pork and make sure it's at least 145°F (63°C). If it's not, place the lid back on and cook for another 2 to 3 minutes, depending on the thickness of your pork chops.

Remove the pork chops from the pot and let them rest on a plate.

Hit SAUTÉ to boil the sauce, whisking occasionally, until it reduces by half or coats the back of a spoon and is a thick glaze, for 5 to 10 minutes.

Serve the pork chops with a generous amount of glaze on top, over the herbed quinoa.

NOTE: Apricot jam will do in a pinch.

Sun-Dried Tomato and Greek Herbed Roast

Sun-dried tomatoes may be my favorite fruit, so when a comfort classic like roast includes them, I know I'll be hooked. Spicing up a roast with more than the typical carrots and onions sounded like a fun way to twist things up. Juicy, tender and full of basil, oregano and dill, this delicious pork may have you craving roast more often than just Sunday meals. You'll notice I use a pork roast—we cannot do beef, and I find that pork can mimic the texture of a typical beef roast and absorb the flavors just as well. If you can and want to, you can use a beef roast, such as chuck, instead.

SERVES 4

½ cup (120 ml) water + 2 tsp (4 g) chicken bouillon powder (or ½ cup [120 ml] chicken broth)

½ cup (55 g) sun-dried tomatoes packed in oil

1 tsp red wine vinegar

3 cloves garlic, minced

1 large red onion, peeled and sliced thinly into half-moons

1 (3- to 4-lb [1.4- to 1.8-kg]) boneless pork roast, cut into 6 equal pieces

2½ tsp (16 g) kosher salt

½ tsp freshly ground black pepper

1 tbsp (2 g) dried basil

1 tbsp (3 g) dried oregano

⅛ tsp dried dill

Dairy-Free Garlic Parsley Mashed Potatoes (page 71), for serving

Place your water and bouillon mixture, tomatoes and their oil, red wine vinegar, garlic and onion in your Instant Pot.

Place the pieces of the roast on top. Next, sprinkle your salt, pepper, basil, oregano and dill over the meat.

Close the lid and move the valve to SEALING. Use the PRESSURE button to set your Instant Pot to high pressure. Hit MANUAL and use the plus and minus buttons to reach 60 minutes.

Once the timer is done, move the valve to VENTING to quickly release the pressure.

Remove the pork from the pot and discard any fat. Shred the meat. If desired, pour the juices through a de-greaser to remove some of the fat from the sauce. Place the shredded meat back into the pot and stir to coat with the sauce.

Serve the shredded meat over the mashed potatoes with a generous drizzle of the sauce and the tomatoes and onion.

Classic Sunday Roast

While I was growing up, my mom would make a roast almost every single Sunday and throw a packet of Lipton Onion Soup on top to flavor it. Oh, how I've missed it since my son can't do beef and those packets have wheat in them. I've finally figured out a recipe with a similar taste, and my own mother says she actually prefers this (gasp!). What's extra nice is that this spice mix makes a double batch—so you can work once and have the roast twice! You'll see I use a pork roast, but if you can do beef, feel free to use that instead. Also, I find that beef broth is usually richer than chicken broth, so since my son cannot have beef, I use a vegan beef bouillon. If you can have beef, feel free to use a regular beef bouillon—just check its label for wheat or other top-8 allergens.

SERVES 4

Salt and pepper

1 (2- to 3-lb [905-g to 1.4-kg]) boneless pork roast, cut into 6 pieces, fat on

8 cubes vegan beef bouillon powder

6 tbsp (41 g) dried minced onion

2 tsp (5 g) onion powder

⅛ tsp crushed celery seeds

⅛ tsp sugar

⅛ tsp red pepper flakes

2 cloves garlic, minced (about 1 tsp)

1 cup (235 ml) water

1 bay leaf

Dairy-Free Garlic Parsley Mashed Potatoes (page 71), for serving

Salt and pepper your pork pieces generously and place them in your Instant Pot.

In a small bowl, stir together your bouillon, dried onion, onion powder, celery seeds, sugar and red pepper flakes. If your bouillon cubes are too firm to crumble, transfer this mixture to a blender and blend. Reserve half of the mixture for later use. Pour the remaining spice mixture over the pork. Place the garlic, water and bay leaf in the Instant Pot.

Close the lid and move the valve to SEALING. Use the PRESSURE button to set your Instant Pot to high pressure. Hit MANUAL and use the plus and minus buttons to reach 60 minutes.

When the timer is done, move the valve to VENTING to quickly release the pressure. Remove the roast from the pot and cut off and discard the fat. Discard the bay leaf. Shred the pork and return it to the juices in the pot, stirring to coat.

Taste and adjust the salt and pepper as needed. Serve the shredded pork and juices over mashed potatoes.

Chicken Taco Salad

Back when I could pick up any store-bought mix without thinking about it, we'd have ground beef with a taco seasoning packet for a taco salad. The silver lining to having to make things from scratch is that you realize how much *better* meals can taste. Instead of being dry crumbles, this moist mixture is splendidly seasoned. If you're not a salad fan, feel free to use this inside taco shells instead. It really is the best ground taco mixture! We use ground chicken since we can't do beef. I find it's cheaper and has less strong a taste than turkey—if you can use ground beef, or if you prefer turkey, those can all be swapped out.

SERVES 4

MEAT MIXTURE

1 tbsp (15 ml) olive oil

1 red onion, finely chopped

2 tbsp (15 g) chili powder

3 cloves garlic, minced (about 1½ tsp [4.5 g])

1 lb (455 g) ground chicken

1 (8-oz [225-g]) can tomato sauce

1 tsp chicken bouillon powder

2 tsp (10 ml) cider vinegar

1 tbsp (15 g) packed light brown sugar

SALAD

Fresh greens of choice (we use romaine), chopped

Fresh cilantro

Olives, halved

Tomatoes, diced

Canned black beans, drained and rinsed

Fresh lime wedges

Dairy-free cheese (optional)

Avocado

Tortilla chips, crushed

Place your olive oil, onion, chili powder, garlic, ground chicken, tomato sauce, bouillon, cider vinegar and brown sugar in your Instant Pot. Stir well to break up the ground chicken.

Close the lid and move the valve to SEALING. Use the pressure button to set your Instant Pot to high pressure. Hit MANUAL and use the plus and minus buttons to reach 5 minutes.

Once the timer is done, move the valve to VENTING to quickly release the pressure.

Stir the ingredients to redistribute. If you would like a thicker sauce, hit SAUTÉ and reduce until the sauce thickens to your liking.

To serve as a salad, place the meat mixture on top of a bed of greens with your salad toppings of choice.

If there are leftovers, keep the meat mixture separate in an airtight container for 1 to 2 days.

Vegan, Nut- & Gluten-Free Mac 'n' Cheese

The only vegan, gluten-free mac 'n' cheese my son had ever had looked like a big glop of fake cheese and was expensive and hard to find. I didn't know if he'd ever enjoy this childhood staple. When I wrote out my table of contents, I put this down and thought—welp, if there's ever a time to figure it out, maybe this is it. Finding a cheese sauce that was dairy-free and that didn't use nuts was a feat. I am so proud of this, and even those who can have dairy say it's a great sauce. This is one of my proudest accomplishments in this book! This is way better than the regular mac 'n' cheese because it also has hidden potatoes and carrots. Extra winning! And speaking of winning, I find this makes more cheese than I need to cover the pasta, so I like to save some for either my Quinoa Nachos (page 27), or to top my broccoli!

SERVES 4

1 tbsp (15 ml) olive oil

2 tsp (12 g) salt, divided

6 cups (1.4 L) plus 1 tbsp (15 ml) water, divided

12 oz (340 g) small gluten-free pasta of choice

1¾ cups (193 g) peeled, chopped potato (about 2 medium russets)

½ cup (65 g) peeled, chopped carrot (about 1 medium or large carrot)

2 tbsp (28 g) vegan butter

3 cloves garlic, minced (about 1½ tsp [4.5 g])

½ cup (118 ml) unsweetened rice milk

½ cup (120 ml) vegetable broth (or ½ cup [120 ml] water + 1 tsp vegetable bouillon powder)

1½ tsp (4 g) onion powder

¾ tsp paprika

¼ cup (32 g) nutritional yeast

3 tbsp (24 g) cornstarch or arrowroot powder

2 tbsp (30 ml) fresh lemon juice

4 oz (115 g) dairy-free cream cheese

Freshly ground black pepper (optional)

Place your olive oil, ½ teaspoon of salt, 5 cups (1.2 L) of the water and the pasta in your Instant Pot. Close the lid and move the valve to SEALING. Use the PRESSURE button to set your Instant Pot to high pressure. Hit MANUAL and use the plus and minus buttons to reach 4 minutes.

Once the timer is done, move the valve to VENTING to quickly release the pressure. Open the lid. Remove and drain the pasta, and set aside.

There's no need to wash the Instant Pot; simply add the 1 cup (250 ml) of water to the pot. Place your trivet on top. If you have a 6-inch (15-cm) cake pan, place the potato, carrot and 1 tablespoon (15 ml) of water in the cake pan. Cover the top tightly with aluminum foil and set it on the trivet. If you do not have a cake pan, make an aluminum foil packet that is tightly sealed with the potatoes and carrot in the middle of it, and set it on the trivet. Close the lid and move the valve to SEALING. Hit MANUAL and use the plus and minus buttons to reach 8 minutes.

Once the timer is done, move the valve to VENTING to quickly release the pressure.

In a high-quality blender, combine the cooked potato and carrot with the remaining 1½ teaspoons (9 g) of salt, vegan butter, garlic, rice milk, broth, onion powder, paprika, nutritional yeast, cornstarch, lemon juice and dairy-free cream cheese. Blend until everything is smooth.

You can pour the sauce on the pasta as is, until it is covered to your liking. Or, if you like it thicker, you can pour the sauce back into the Instant Pot, hit SAUTÉ and boil it until it thickens to your liking. Top the cheesy pasta with freshly ground black pepper, if so desired.

Smothered Pork Chops

Calling all my pork lovers—this is for you! Pork chops cooked in bacon grease with bacon crumbled on top? Say it ain't so. This indulgent meal will satisfy any meat lover in your life. (This is also great for Father's Day!) Serve with a side of potatoes and it's the quintessential meat and potato pairing. If you can't do Worcestershire sauce, feel free to use coconut aminos instead.

SERVES 4

1 (12-oz [340-g]) package bacon

1 large yellow onion, cut into half-moons

4 boneless pork chops, about ½" (1.3 cm) thick

½ tsp salt

½ tsp freshly ground black pepper

4 oz (115 g) mushrooms, sliced

1 cup (235 ml) water + 2 tsp (4 g) chicken bouillon powder (or 1 cup [235 ml] chicken broth)

1 tbsp (15 ml) gluten-free Worcestershire sauce or coconut aminos

2 bay leaves

2 tbsp (30 ml) cold water

2 tbsp (16 g) cornstarch or arrowroot powder

3 cloves garlic, finely chopped (about 1½ tsp [4.5 g])

1 tbsp (15 ml) cider vinegar

Dairy-Free Garlic Parsley Mashed Potatoes (page 71), for serving

Using kitchen shears, cut your bacon into bite-size pieces and place them in your Instant Pot. Hit SAUTÉ and, stirring frequently with a wooden spoon, cook the bacon until crispy, 5 to 7 minutes. Transfer the bacon to a paper towel–lined plate, leaving half, or more to preference, of the bacon grease in the pot. Add the onion and sauté, stirring frequently, until it is translucent, 3 to 5 minutes. Turn off the SAUTÉ function.

Place your pork chops, salt, pepper, mushrooms, water and bouillon mixture, Worcestershire and bay leaves in the Instant Pot. Close the lid and move the valve to SEALING. Use the PRESSURE button to set your Instant Pot to high pressure. Hit the MANUAL button and use the plus and minus buttons to reach 10 minutes.

Once the timer is done, allow the pressure to release naturally (this takes around 10 minutes).

Once you're able to open the lid, transfer the pork chops to a plate to rest. In a small bowl, whisk together the cold water and cornstarch. Add the garlic, vinegar and slurry to the Instant Pot. Hit SAUTÉ and bring the mixture to a boil. Boil for 1 minute. Turn off the SAUTÉ function, discard the bay leaves and return the pork chops to the sauce, stirring to coat.

Serve the pork chops over mashed potatoes with a drizzle of the sauce and the crumbled bacon on top.

TWO

Stress-Free Sides

Everyone wants that comforting side dish, those mountainous piles of mashed potatoes or the crisp bite of corn on the cob—but we don't want butter dripping from either of those. Finding sides that are dairy- and gluten-free, let alone free of the top-8 allergens, can be tough. My motto is "Give up ingredients, but don't give up awesomeness." The only thing you're really giving up here is more dirty dishes and more time—which I don't think anyone minds.

Now with the Instant Pot, my potatoes can be fork-tender in the time it used to take me to boil water. I can use up my dried beans, and make vegetables without having to wait and watch to see whether something simmers over when I'm tied up with the main dish. The Instant Pot gives you the best flavor in a fraction of the time to assist your main dishes and round out your meal with satisfying sides, such as grains, vegetables and legumes. I love to have side dishes—it's a great way to make sure there's plenty to eat (hello, growing boys!). In fact, my ideal dinner scenario is a main plus two sides. I so enjoy making side dishes in the Instant Pot that I actually have two Instant Pots now! That way I can prepare my main and side dish at the time same. Some might call it obsessed, but I've heard "obsessed" is another word for "committed." Ha!

Speaking of time saving, my bean recipes make more than enough for one night, so I freeze half of them—thus not having to worry about a side dish at a later date. Cook once (and even hardly at that!) and eat twice is the motto of a happy, busy mom.

Cilantro, Garlic & Lime Rice & Beans

Do I dare say this is better than Chipotle's? Why, yes, yes, I do! Your beans and rice are all enveloped together in the bold flavors of garlic and lime. This is a crowd-pleasing side to any Southwestern or Mexican dish, or it can be used as a filling in any taco or burrito. My husband is Haitian, and in the Caribbean, rice and beans are a staple. He loves this dish and gets sad when it's gone every time. Rice and beans are so inexpensive and super filling, making them the ideal side dish!

SERVES 4

1½ cups (293 g) long-grain white rice, rinsed

1½ cups (255 ml) water

2 tsp (4 g) chicken bouillon powder

1 tbsp (15 ml) olive oil

1¼ tsp (7.5 g) salt

1 bay leaf

Zest of 1 lime

⅓ cup (13 g) finely chopped fresh cilantro

2 tbsp (30 ml) fresh lime juice

2 cloves garlic, minced (about 1 tsp)

1 (15-oz [425-g]) can black beans, drained and rinsed well

Place your rice, water, bouillon, olive oil, salt, bay leaf and lime zest in your Instant Pot. Close the lid and move the valve to SEALING. Use the PRESSURE button to set your Instant Pot to high pressure. Hit the MANUAL button and use the plus and minus buttons to reach 5 minutes.

Once the timer is done, allow the pressure to naturally release for 5 minutes. After the display reads "L:05" you can move the valve to VENTING to finish releasing any leftover pressure.

Open the lid and stir in the cilantro, lime juice, garlic and black beans. Discard the bay leaf. Stir well and serve with your favorite tacos or other Southwestern or Mexican main dishes.

Lemon Herbed Quinoa

If you are not familiar with quinoa, say hello to your new best friend. It's an edible seed, and it reminds me a lot of a smaller couscous (anyone else miss that wheat-based grain?). It has a great, al dente bite and is very mild, which makes it great for taking on flavorings. It also has a ton of protein! We love to swap in this side when we get sick of rice. Adding some herbs, lemon juice and olive oil makes this so yummy that my kids will eat it as a snack with just a spoon!

SERVES 4

1½ cups (260 g) uncooked quinoa, rinsed

2 cups (475 ml) water

2 tbsp (4 g) chicken bouillon powder

1 tbsp (15 ml) olive oil

1 tbsp (15 ml) fresh lemon juice

1 tsp dried basil

½ tsp dried oregano

½ tsp dried parsley

¼ tsp dried rosemary

Place your quinoa, water, bouillon, olive oil, lemon juice, basil, oregano, parsley and rosemary in your Instant Pot. Close the lid and move the valve to SEALING. Use the PRESSURE button to set your Instant Pot to high pressure. Hit the MANUAL button and use the plus and minus buttons to reach 1 minute.

Once the timer is done, allow the pressure to release naturally for 10 minutes. Once the display shows "L:10," you can move the valve to VENTING to finish releasing any leftover pressure.

Open the lid and stir. Serve as a complement to any main dish—especially my Apricot-Glazed Pork Chops (page 51).

Salsa Mexican Rice

Rice is kicked up a notch when it's cooked in salsa. It's an easy hack that imparts tons of flavors without your having to measure out spices. With notes of bell peppers, loads of tomato-y goodness and cumin, this Salsa Mexican Rice is the ideal side for grilled meats, taco nights or any Southwestern dish.

SERVES 4

1 tbsp (15 ml) olive oil

1½ tsp (4 g) onion powder

1 tsp ground cumin

1½ cups (293 g) uncooked white rice

1¾ cups (415 ml) chicken broth (or 1¾ cups [415 ml] water + 4 tsp [8 g] chicken bouillon powder)

1 cup (260 g) chunky salsa

Juice of ½ lime (about 1½ tbsp [22.5 ml] juice)

Freshly chopped cilantro, for garnish (optional)

Place your olive oil, onion powder, cumin, rice, broth and salsa in your Instant Pot. Close the lid and move the valve to SEALING. Use the PRESSURE button to set your Instant Pot to high pressure. Hit MANUAL and use the plus and minus buttons to reach 3 minutes.

Once the timer is done, move the valve to VENTING to quickly release the pressure.

Open the lid and add the lime juice. Stir.

Top with cilantro, if so desired, and serve warm.

Dairy-Free Garlic Parsley Mashed Potatoes

Who says you need loads of milk, cream or butter to have melt-in-your-mouth mashed potatoes? Rice milk, chicken broth and olive oil do the same trick for soft mountains of creamy potatoes. Whenever we have family gatherings, my sister—who can eat anything—asks for *me* to bring the mashed potatoes. She says she likes mine better! Booyah. The garlic and parsley add an extra layer of flavor that will accompany any roast or cut of meat. Full of craters to hold gravy, drippings and sauces, this is one side dish we have on repeat and never tire of! Seriously, what are you waiting for? Dog-ear the page now!

SERVES 4

2½ lb (1.1 kg) russet potatoes (about 7 medium potatoes)

2 tsp (12 g) salt, divided

2 tbsp (30 ml) olive oil

3 to 4 tbsp (45 to 60 ml) unsweetened rice milk (depending on how creamy you like your mashed potatoes)

1 tsp dried parsley

6 cloves garlic, minced (about 1 tbsp [10 g])

2 tsp (4 g) chicken bouillon powder

Freshly ground black pepper, for garnish

Vegan butter, for serving

Peel and dice your potatoes into small cubes. Add them to your Instant Pot along with enough water to cover the potatoes. Add 1 teaspoon of the salt.

Close the lid and move the valve to SEALING. Use the PRESSURE button to set your Instant Pot to high pressure. Hit MANUAL and use the plus and minus buttons to reach 8 minutes.

Once the timer is done, move the valve to VENTING to quickly release the pressure and open the lid.

Drain the potatoes. Place them in a bowl and add the remaining teaspoon of salt as well as the olive oil, rice milk, parsley, garlic and bouillon.

Using an electric mixer, beat the potatoes until they're smooth and creamy, adding more rice milk if necessary to reach your desired creaminess. Taste and adjust the salt as desired. Add pepper to taste and a dollop of vegan butter. Serve hot.

Leftovers keep well for 2 to 3 days in an airtight container. Best served with any of my roasts or turkey breast.

Cheese-Free Scalloped Potatoes

If you think you need cheese to make creamy, comforting and flavorful scalloped potatoes, you, my friend, are wrong. Gluten-free flour helps create the thick, creamy texture and garlic, onion and chives give the potatoes all the flavor they need. I make these every Christmas and Easter for my extended family and they're the first thing to go! I sometimes even make these with cubed ham steak mixed in for an easy, one-dish meal the kids enjoy. I used to make them in the oven, but they'd take 90 minutes to soften completely. I love that this is quicker, and it's great to do a double batch, since the Instant Pot can only fit a small container.

SERVES 4

1 cup (235 ml) water

4 small to medium russet potatoes

3 tbsp (45 ml) olive oil

¼ cup (30 g) gluten-free flour of choice

1¼ cups (285 ml) chicken or vegetable broth

¼ cup (60 g) vegan mayonnaise

1 tsp salt

1½ tsp (4 g) minced garlic (about 3 cloves)

1 yellow onion, chopped finely

Sea salt and pepper, to taste

Fresh chives, chopped, for garnish

Place the water in the bottom of your Instant Pot. Set the trivet on top.

Thinly and evenly slice your potatoes. I prefer to use a food processor so that they're uniform and quickly sliced.

In a bowl, combine your olive oil, gluten-free flour, broth, mayonnaise, salt, garlic, potatoes and onion. Stir well to incorporate everything.

Fill a 6-inch (15-cm)-diameter cake pan (or any pan that will fit on top of your trivet) with the potato mixture. You will have some left over, which you can pressure cook separately or toss. Cover the top of the pan tightly with aluminum foil.

Set the covered pan on top of the trivet. Close the lid and move the valve to SEALING. Use the PRESSURE button to set your Instant Pot to high pressure. Hit MANUAL and use the plus and minus button to reach 30 minutes.

When the timer is up, move the valve to VENTING to quickly release the pressure and open the lid. Carefully lift out the pan and take off the aluminum foil, being careful of the hot steam.

You can either serve this as is, or place the pan in your oven under the broiler for a few minutes to crisp and brown the top.

Sprinkle sea salt and pepper on top, along with chives.

Wild Rice, Cranberry & Sweet Potato Pilaf

Since we can't do stuffing, I wanted a Thanksgiving-inspired side dish that was studded with textures and colors. The heartiness of wild rice paired with soft potato and the bursts of sweet tang from dried cranberries gives this multidimensional side dish two thumbs way, way up. If you can do nuts, feel free to swap in pecans or walnuts instead of sunflower seeds for the fun bite of crunch.

SERVES 4

2 cups (473 ml) water

4 tsp (8 g) chicken bouillon powder

1 cup (178 g) uncooked wild rice blend (unseasoned)

1 tbsp (15 ml) olive oil

½ tsp dried parsley

½ tsp dried oregano

½ tsp salt

¼ tsp dried thyme

¼ tsp dried rosemary

¾ cup (120 g) chopped red onion (about ½ onion)

1½ cups (165 g) diced sweet potato, bite-size pieces

⅓ cup (40 g) dried cranberries

⅓ cup (48 g) salted sunflower seeds

Place your water, bouillon, rice blend, olive oil, parsley, oregano, salt, thyme, rosemary and onion in your Instant Pot. Close the lid and move the valve to SEALING. Use the PRESSURE button to set your Instant Pot to high pressure. Hit MANUAL and use the plus and minus buttons to reach 28 minutes.

Once the timer is done, move the valve to venting to quickly release the pressure.

Open the lid and add the sweet potato. Close the lid again. Move the valve to SEALING and use the plus and minus buttons to reach 2 minutes.

Once the timer is done, move the valve to venting to quickly release the pressure.

Open the lid and stir in the dried cranberries and sunflower seeds before serving.

Dairy-Free Sweet Potato Casserole

Instead of using cream as a liquid in this casserole, I use apple juice—which gives it the moisture it needs, plus some natural sweetener. With hints of cinnamon and topped with the classic marshmallow, this top 8–free holiday staple is one you'll make year after year. The Instant Pot is perfect for softening sweet potatoes and does it in a jiffy. To ensure the creamiest casserole, make sure you peel past the white layer of the sweet potato; then use an electric mixer, which will grab any remaining strings. If you want, you can even make this ahead of time, and let it sit on WARM—just wait to add the marshmallows until you're ready to serve! For a fun way to switch this up, you can swap in orange juice for apple juice for a citrus kick.

SERVES 4

4 to 5 sweet potatoes, peeled and roughly cubed

⅓ cup (80 ml) apple juice

1 tsp ground cinnamon

½ tsp ground nutmeg

½ tsp salt

½ cup (115 g) light brown sugar

2 tsp (10 ml) vanilla extract

2 cups (100 g) mini marshmallows, or to your preference (vegan if needed)

Place your sweet potatoes, apple juice, cinnamon, nutmeg, salt and brown sugar in your Instant Pot. Close the lid and move the valve to SEALING. Use the PRESSURE button to set your Instant Pot to high pressure. Hit MANUAL and use the plus and minus buttons to reach 8 minutes.

After the timer is done, move the valve to VENTING to quickly release the pressure.

Open the lid and use an electric mixer to puree the mixture. Stir in the vanilla. Top with the marshmallows. Remove the Instant Pot's metal insert and place it in the oven set to BROIL. Watch carefully and broil for 1 to 2 minutes, or until the top is nice and golden brown. Serve immediately.

Southwest Black Beans

These black beans are so flavorful, they smack you in the mouth. Garlic, oregano and a squeeze of lime make this side dish a contender as the star of the dinner show. With no soaking required, these once dried black beans come to life with the ease of the Instant Pot. Warning: these may make you hate canned beans for life, so proceed with caution!

SERVES 4

1 lb (455 g) dried black beans, rinsed

1 tbsp (15 ml) olive oil

1 yellow onion, diced

4 cups (945 ml) water

3 tbsp (18 g) chicken bouillon powder

½ tsp ground cumin

½ tsp ground coriander

½ tsp dried oregano

1 tsp salt, or more to taste

1 bay leaf

4 cloves garlic, minced (about 2 tsp [6 g])

Juice of 1 lime (about 3 tbsp [45 ml])

Freshly ground black pepper, to taste

Place your black beans, olive oil, onion, water, bouillon, cumin, coriander, oregano, salt and bay leaf in your Instant Pot. Close the lid and move the valve to SEALING. Use the PRESSURE button to set your Instant Pot to high pressure. Hit MANUAL and use the plus and minus buttons to reach 35 minutes.

Once the timer is done, move the valve to VENTING to quickly release the pressure.

Open the lid and stir in the garlic and lime juice. Adjust the salt and pepper to your liking. Discard the bay leaf.

Serve with your favorite Mexican or Southwestern dish. Once the beans are cool, they freeze wonderfully. I find we eat about half, and then I save the rest in the freezer for another busy night!

NOTES: Because of the intense heating of the unsoaked beans, you will find that some shriveled ones float to the top. These will not be as tender, and you can discard them. If that bothers you, and you want prettier beans without shriveling, then feel free to soak them in water overnight! Simply drain the soaked beans and follow the recipe as normal.

Bacon & Brown Sugar Baked Beans

A grilling and summer staple, baked beans are a sweet and zesty side dish that packs a tasty punch. Bacon, vinegar, liquid smoke, brown sugar and molasses all impart a delicious blanket of flavor. Whenever I'm asked to bring a side dish to summer get-togethers, this is what I bring! As with all of my beans, this requires no soaking and makes enough to freeze for a later date (because we all know how summer days are jam packed!). Salty from the bacon and sweet from the brown sugar and molasses, this is the yin to your yang. As always, you can omit the Worcestershire, if necessary, as it contains fish.

SERVES 4

1 (12-oz [340-g]) package bacon

1 large red onion, diced small

1 green bell pepper, seeded and diced small

1 lb (455 g) dried great northern beans, rinsed

¼ tsp salt

¼ tsp freshly ground black pepper

3¾ cups (885 ml) water

1 tbsp (15 ml) cider vinegar

1 tbsp (15 ml) gluten-free Worcestershire sauce

1 tsp liquid smoke

⅓ cup (75 g) light brown sugar

½ cup (170 g) molasses

4 cloves garlic, minced

8 oz (225 g) tomato sauce

¼ cup (60 ml) cold water

3 tbsp (24 g) cornstarch or arrowroot powder

Using kitchen shears, cut your bacon into bite-size pieces and place them in your Instant Pot. Hit SAUTÉ and cook the bacon until crisp, 5 to 7 minutes. Remove the bacon from the pot and set aside on a paper towel–lined plate to absorb any excess grease.

Remove all but about 2 tablespoons (30 ml) of the bacon grease. Turn off the SAUTÉ function and add your onion, bell pepper, beans, salt, black pepper, water, vinegar and Worcestershire. Use the PRESSURE button to set your Instant Pot to high pressure. Close the lid and hit MANUAL; then use the plus and minus buttons to reach 45 minutes.

When the timer is done, let the pressure release naturally (about 10 minutes).

Open the lid and add your liquid smoke, brown sugar, molasses, garlic and tomato sauce. Hit SAUTÉ and bring to a boil, stirring frequently. In a small bowl, whisk together the water and cornstarch. Once the sauce is boiling, add the slurry. Allow the mixture to boil, stirring frequently, for 3 to 5 minutes, or until it reaches your desired thickness (the sauce will continue to thicken as it cools).

Sesame-Free Hummus

This is a delicious and easy way to use up your store of dried garbanzo beans (a.k.a. chickpeas). No soaking is required! This from-scratch hummus has extra kicks of flavor not only due to the sriracha but thanks to garlic and cumin. Dried beans are so inexpensive and make so much more than what you get for paying for hummus! This is great as a snack with gluten-free chips, as an appetizer with a vegetable tray or as part of a veggie-filled wrap. My hummus-enthusiast friend says that I've ruined her—that all store-bought hummus now tastes to her, and I quote, "like dirt."

SERVES 4

8 oz (255 g) dried garbanzo beans

2 tsp (12 g) salt, divided

½ tsp sriracha sauce, or more to taste

¼ cup (60 ml) olive oil

¼ cup (60 ml) water

¼ cup (60 ml) fresh lemon juice

1 tsp red wine vinegar

2 cloves garlic, minced (about 1 tsp)

1 tsp ground cumin

Tortilla chips or gluten-free crackers and veggies, for serving

Place your dried beans in your Instant Pot and add enough water to cover the beans by at least an inch (2.5 cm). Add 1 teaspoon of the salt.

Close the lid and move the valve to SEALING. Use the PRESSURE button to set your Instant Pot to high pressure. Hit MANUAL and use the plus and minus buttons to reach 45 minutes.

Once the timer is done, move the valve to VENTING to quickly release the pressure. Drain the beans.

Place the sriracha, olive oil, water, lemon juice, vinegar, garlic, cumin and the remaining teaspoon of salt in a blender or food processor. Add the beans. Blend until smooth and creamy.

Serve with tortilla chips or your favorite gluten-free crackers and veggies.

Thick & Creamy Refried Beans

I never knew I could love refried beans as much as I do now. I'd often skip them before, thinking they were just a layer of blandness. Now, I see them as the comfort food of Mexican cuisine. They're the mashed potatoes of the Latin world, no soaking required and filled with flavor. I sleep well at night knowing I have a batch in the fridge ready to go. You'll be surprised how you will become an advocate for these refried beans, too.

SERVES 4

1 tbsp (15 ml) olive oil

1 yellow onion, roughly chopped

½ jalapeño pepper, seeded and roughly chopped

16 oz (455 g) dried pinto beans, rinsed

4 cups (945 ml) water

2½ tbsp (15 g) chicken bouillon powder

1½ tsp (9 g) salt, or more to taste

2 tbsp (30 ml) white vinegar

4 cloves garlic, minced (about 2 tsp [6 g])

Freshly ground black pepper, to taste

Place your olive oil, onion, jalapeño, beans, water, bouillon, salt and vinegar in your Instant Pot. Close the lid and move the valve to SEALING. Use the PRESSURE button to set your Instant Pot to high pressure. Hit MANUAL and use the plus and minus buttons to reach 45 minutes.

Once the timer is done, move the valve to VENTING to quickly release the pressure.

Pour the entire mixture (beans, water and veggies), in two batches, into a high-quality blender and blend to your desired texture (I prefer mine silky smooth). A food processor or immersion blender will also work. Stir in the garlic. Taste and adjust the salt and pepper to preference.

NOTE: This freezes great. I like to use half of the batch for dinner (perfect for any Mexican or Southwestern dish) and some bean burritos that week and freeze the other in a resealable plastic bag.

Honey Cinnamon Carrots

My mom was the OG of pressure cookers and had a stove-top version while I was growing up. She frequently made glazed carrots and I loved them as a child. It's fun to put my own spin on them by using honey instead of brown sugar and a touch of cinnamon to give them an almost candied taste. My kids will eat these plain and think they're getting a treat instead of a side dish! This is also a wonderful holiday staple. I've found different people like different textures for their carrots; if you enjoy more of a bite, cook them for three minutes, or for softer, do up to five minutes. You do you!

SERVES 4

1 (2-lb [905-g]) bag baby carrots

½ cup (120 ml) water

¼ tsp salt

1 tbsp (15 ml) coconut oil, melted

¼ cup (85 g) honey

¾ tsp ground cinnamon

Place your carrots, water and salt in your Instant Pot.

Close the lid and move the valve to SEALING. Use the PRESSURE button to set your Instant Pot to high pressure. Hit MANUAL and use the plus and minus buttons to reach 3 to 5 minutes (see headnote).

Meanwhile, in a small bowl, combine the coconut oil, honey and cinnamon. Stir well and set aside.

When the timer is done, move the valve to VENTING to quickly release the pressure.

Open the lid and drain the water. Pour the honey mixture over the drained carrots and stir well to coat.

Broccoli & "Cheese"

If parents want their kids to eat broccoli, it seems like they'll slather it in cheese. This was never an option for us, until I recently discovered my life-changing Mac 'n' Cheese (page 59). When I noticed I had cheese sauce left over, I realized I could finally have that coveted cascade of cheese poured over broccoli. The mountainous pile in this picture was literally eaten as a snack by my children all in one sitting. Parents all over the vegan world, rejoice!

SERVES 4

2 cups (470 ml) water, divided

2 to 3 medium heads broccoli, cut into florets

CHEESE SAUCE

1¾ cups (165 g) peeled, diced potato (about 2 medium russets)

½ cup (65 g) peeled, diced carrot (about 1 medium to large carrot)

2 tbsp (28 g) vegan butter

3 cloves garlic, minced (about 1½ tsp [4.5 g])

½ cup (118 ml) unsweetened rice milk

½ cup (120 ml) vegetable broth (or ½ cup [120 ml] water + 1 tsp vegetable bouillon powder)

1½ tsp (4 g) onion powder

1½ tsp (9 g) salt

¾ tsp paprika

¼ cup (32 g) nutritional yeast

3 tbsp (24 g) cornstarch or arrowroot powder

2 tbsp (30 ml) fresh lemon juice

4 oz (115 g) dairy-free cream cheese

Place 1 cup (235 ml) of the water in your Instant Pot. Place the trivet on top of the water and a steamer basket on top of the trivet. Fill the trivet with the broccoli.

Close the lid and move the valve to SEALING. Use the PRESSURE button to set your Instant Pot to high pressure. Hit MANUAL and use the plus and minus buttons to reach 0 minutes. This will allow it come to pressure and then end—which is the perfect amount of cooking time for something as tender as broccoli.

Move the valve to VENTING to quickly release the pressure. Drain the broccoli and transfer it to a covered bowl to keep it warm.

Add the remaining cup (235 ml) of water to the Instant Pot. Place your trivet on top. If you have a 6-inch (15-cm) round cake pan, place the potatoes and carrots in that, cover the top tightly with aluminum foil and set it on the trivet. If you do not have a small cake pan, make an aluminum foil packet that is tightly sealed with the potatoes and carrots in the middle of it and set it on the trivet. Close the lid and move the valve to SEALING. Hit MANUAL and use the plus and minus buttons to reach 8 minutes.

Once the timer is done, move the valve to VENTING to quickly release the pressure.

Place the cooked potatoes and carrots as well as the vegan butter, garlic, rice milk, broth, onion powder, salt, paprika, nutritional yeast, cornstarch, lemon juice and dairy-free cream cheese in a high-quality blender or food processor. Blend until everything is smooth.

You can either pour the sauce on the broccoli, until it is covered to your liking, or if you like the sauce thicker, pour it back into the Instant Pot, hit SAUTÉ and boil it until it thickens to your liking.

Use the leftover cheese to pour over cooked pasta or Quinoa Nachos (page 27), or freeze it.

Easiest Corn on the Cob

Hi, my name is Megan and I suffer from being impatient. I have a hard time waiting for water to boil. Is that just me? Corn takes only a few minutes to cook, so it used to kill me that it'd take quadruple that time just to wait for the water to be hot enough. I tried making it in the microwave to save time, but that made my whole house smell like dirt-filled husks. This has to be my new favorite, time-saving way of making a summer staple! The texture is bite-tastic and you don't have to turn your kitchen into a humid cave waiting for a large pot of water to boil. The summer corn gods smile approvingly.

SERVES 4

1½ cups (355 ml) water

1 tbsp (13 g) sugar

3 to 4 ears of corn, husk and silk removed

Vegan butter, for serving

Salt, for serving

Place your water and sugar in your Instant Pot. Set the trivet on top of the water.

Place the corn, either whole or cut in half so it will fit, on the trivet.

Close the lid and move the valve to SEALING. Use the PRESSURE button to set your Instant Pot to high pressure. Hit MANUAL and use the plus and minus buttons to reach 2 minutes.

Once the timer is done, move the valve to VENTING to quickly release the pressure.

Remove the corn (careful, it is hot!) and serve warm with your favorite vegan butter and salt on top.

Two-Minute Lemon Asparagus

I live for spring asparagus season and it's such a welcome rotation after a long winter of typical vegetables. The tender stalks of asparagus are *made* for some freshly squeezed lemon, pepper and salt. No need for something fancy when these essential ingredients make the asparagus sing. Well . . . of course I had to add just a *titch* more flavor and sprinkle on some garlic salt to really make it pop. I can't deny the flavor-holic in me.

SERVES 4

1 cup (235 ml) water

1 lb (455 g) asparagus, trimmed

Fresh lemon, for squeezing

¼ tsp salt

¼ tsp freshly ground black pepper

¼ tsp garlic salt

Place the water in the bottom of your Instant Pot. Place the trivet on top of the water. Set the trimmed asparagus on top of the trivet. (If you find they're dropping into the water, you can also set the spears in a steamer basket on top of the trivet.)

Close the lid and move the valve to SEALING. Use the PRESSURE button to set your Instant Pot to high pressure. Hit MANUAL and use the plus and minus buttons to reach your desired time. I find that I need 2 minutes if they are thick spears or 1 minute if they are thin.

Once the timer is done, move the valve to VENTING to quickly release the pressure. Open the lid and remove the spears. Drizzle with generous squeezes of fresh lemon juice and sprinkle with the salt, pepper and garlic salt. Best if eaten right away.

THREE

Snappy Soups

I'm always sad to see summer end. Every time the snow flies in Utah, I ask my husband why in the world we haven't moved to a beach in North Carolina yet. The only thing that gets me through the impending cold weather is remembering that fall and winter mean soups! I could have soup every other night from October through April.

You're going to have a hard time deciding which one to try first—especially since these require so much less tending than the stovetop versions, and the Instant Pot softens beans, potatoes and carrots much quicker than the stove ever could. You can even throw in frozen chicken breasts and have the most tender shredded meat floating in delectable broth in no time.

None of these soups uses wheat as a thickener or cheese as a topping, but all are still just as warming and soul soothing. These also needed to be filling on their own, because we can't rely on bread or rolls as part of the meal. These soups will be what help you look forward to the colder weather, too.

If you're craving something thick and hearty, go with my No-Cans-Needed Chicken & Wild Rice Soup (page 99). If you're wanting a bit of spice, you'll go wild for my Green Chile Chicken Enchilada Soup (page 103). And, for a classic meat and potato lovers' meal, you'll love my Potato & Sausage soup (page 100).

Cream-Free Zuppa Toscana

A copycat of Olive Garden's famous soup, this creamy zuppa Toscana is one of my husband's favorites. It's probably because it features not one, but two meats—Italian sausage *and* bacon. Add creamy potatoes, and well, it's a good thing there's some spinach in there so we all don't feel too guilty. Thanks to coconut milk, this is creamy and rich without needing any milk products!

SERVES 4 TO 6

6 slices bacon

1 lb (455 g) Italian sausage

1 yellow onion, diced

4 russet potatoes, peeled and cubed

4 cups (945 ml) water

12 cloves garlic, minced (about 2 tbsp [20 g])

2 tbsp (4 g) chicken bouillon powder

1 cup (30 g) roughly chopped spinach or kale

2 tbsp (16 g) cornstarch or arrowroot powder

⅓ cup (80 ml) cold water

1 cup (235 ml) canned full-fat coconut milk

Salt and pepper, to taste

Using sharp kitchen shears, cut your bacon into bite-size pieces. Place the bacon in your Instant Pot and hit SAUTÉ. Cook until crispy, 5 to 7 minutes. Transfer the cooked bacon to a paper towel–lined plate.

Remove all but 1 tablespoon (15 ml) of the grease from the pot. Add your Italian sausage and cook until browned, 5 to 7 minutes. Then, add your onion and cook until soft. Turn off your Instant Pot.

Next, add your potatoes, water, garlic and chicken bouillon. Close the lid and move the valve to SEALING. Use the PRESSURE button to set your Instant Pot to high pressure. Hit the MANUAL button and use the plus and minus buttons to reach 8 minutes.

When the timer is done, move the valve to VENTING to quickly release the pressure; then open the lid. Add the spinach and hit the SAUTÉ function to bring the mixture to a boil. In a small bowl, whisk together the cornstarch and cold water. Once the soup is boiling, add the slurry. Allow the soup to boil for 1 minute. Turn off your Instant Pot, add your canned coconut milk and stir to incorporate. Add the salt and pepper to taste.

No-Cans-Needed Chicken & Wild Rice Soup

This is, by far, my favorite soup. Probably because it's nostalgic for me, as my mom would make something similar. There is something about the bite of wild rice swimming in a thick broth punctuated by carrots that just feels cozy and right. Unfortunately, she used condensed soup and an Uncle Ben's wild rice packet—which means the soup had both wheat and dairy in it. So, I set out to make the same thing, but by scratch and without milk or wheat products. I have succeeded in replicating my mom's recipe and now my kids will know the pleasure of a creamy bowl of Chicken & Wild Rice Soup. Although, my kids know to leave the leftovers for me, ha!

SERVES 4 TO 6

1 tbsp (15 ml) olive oil

1 yellow onion, diced finely

3 carrots, diced

2 celery ribs, cut into half moons

2 chicken breasts

1 cup (178 g) seasoned long-grain rice and wild rice blend (I use Ankeny Lakes Wild & Ricey)

8 oz (225 g) button mushrooms, sliced

5 cups (1.2 L) water, divided

3½ tbsp (21 g) chicken bouillon powder

3 cloves garlic, minced (about 1½ tsp [4.5 g])

4 oz (115 g) dairy-free cream cheese

Salt and pepper, to taste

Place your olive oil, onion, carrots, celery, chicken breasts, wild rice blend, mushrooms, 4 cups (945 ml) of the water and the bouillon in your Instant Pot. Secure the lid and move the valve to SEALING. Use the PRESSURE button to set your Instant Pot to high pressure. Hit MANUAL and use the plus and minus buttons to reach 25 minutes.

After the timer is done, move the valve to VENTING to quickly release the pressure.

Remove the chicken from the pot, shred it and return it to the pot.

Stir in the garlic.

Place the cream cheese and the remaining cup (235 ml) of water in a blender and blend to a smooth consistency; then add that to the soup.

Give everything a stir. Adjust the salt and pepper to your liking. Serve warm. Leftovers keep well for 2 to 3 days and freeze fabulously!

TIP: I find dairy-free cream cheese doesn't melt well, which is why if you want it completely incorporated you should blend it first.

Potato & Sausage Soup

This is one of the first recipes I made with my Instant Pot. Since then, I've taken it to a neighborhood cook-off. A professional chef was there and even he asked for this recipe! #blushing. It's hearty, it's got classic flavors and it's easy—all the things you'd want for a cold winter day. My kids happily slurp this down and fight for the biggest piece of sausage!

SERVES 4 TO 6

1 tbsp (15 ml) extra virgin olive oil

1 small yellow onion, diced

1 lb (455 g) Italian sausage

2 potatoes, cubed

1 celery rib, diced

2 carrots, diced

1 (15-oz [425-g]) can diced tomatoes, undrained

1 (15-oz [425-g]) can white beans, undrained

4½ cups (1.1 L) chicken broth (or 4½ cups [1.1 L] water + 2½ tbsp [15 g] chicken bouillon powder)

1 tsp dried parsley

Salt and pepper, to taste

Hit SAUTÉ and pour your olive oil in your Instant Pot. Once it's hot, add your onion and cook until it's translucent, 1 to 2 minutes. Next, add your Italian sausage and brown it.

Turn off the SAUTÉ function and add the potatoes, celery, carrots, diced tomatoes, white beans, broth and parsley.

Close the lid; then move the valve to SEALING. Use the PRESSURE button to set your Instant Pot to high pressure. Hit MANUAL and use the plus and minus buttons to reach 10 minutes.

Once the timer is done, move the valve to VENTING to quickly release the pressure. Taste, and adjust the salt and pepper to your liking.

Green Chile Chicken Enchilada Soup

A Tex-Mex soup that is spicy, comforting and crave-worthy, this is a favorite in our house. And, better than that—whenever I go to my best friend's house for dinner, it's often what she's making, too! I've got her obsessed! Filling with two kinds of beans, chicken and chiles, this is great for crumbling some tortilla chips on top for a salty crunch.

SERVES 4 TO 6

1 (16-oz [455-g]) can green enchilada sauce (heat to preference; we do mild)

1 (15-oz [425-g]) can white beans, drained and rinsed

1 (15-oz [425-g]) can black beans, drained and rinsed

2 boneless, skinless chicken breasts

7 oz (198 g) diced fire-roasted green chiles (heat to preference; we do mild)

1 (14.5-oz [415-g]) can fire-roasted diced tomatoes

1 tsp chili powder

1 tbsp (7 g) ground cumin

2 cups (473 ml) chicken broth (or 2 cups [473 ml] water + 4 tsp [8 g] chicken bouillon powder)

4 oz (115 g) dairy-free cream cheese, softened

Salt and pepper, to taste

OPTIONAL TOPPINGS

Fresh cilantro, chopped

Dairy-free sour cream

Fresh lime

Tortilla chips

Place your enchilada sauce, white beans, black beans, chicken, green chiles, tomatoes, chili powder and cumin in your Instant Pot. Close the lid and move the valve to SEALING. Use the PRESSURE button to set your Instant Pot to high pressure. Hit MANUAL, and use the plus and minus buttons to reach 12 minutes.

Once the timer is done, move the valve to VENTING to quickly release the pressure.

Remove the chicken from the pot and shred it; then return it to the pot.

Combine the chicken broth and dairy-free cream cheese in a blender. Blend until smooth.

Pour the cheese mixture into the soup and stir to incorporate. Taste and adjust the salt and pepper to your liking.

Garnish with cilantro and any additional toppings you enjoy.

Vegan & Gluten-Free Minestrone

You'd think I'd remember, but often after eating this, I forget it's vegan because it's so hearty and so filling. If there was ever a soup that didn't need meat, this is it. If you don't need it to be vegan, you can use honey instead of agave. Beans, noodles and loads of veggies make this tasty and textured. The classic Italian herbs oregano and basil, along with balsamic vinegar, make this a rich minestrone that you don't need to go to a restaurant to enjoy. Fast and delicious, this is a soup you'll have on repeat.

SERVES 4 TO 6

2 tbsp (30 ml) olive oil

1 large yellow onion, diced

5 cloves garlic, minced (about 2½ tsp [7.5 g])

2 bay leaves

2 tsp (2 g) dried oregano

1 tbsp (15 ml) balsamic vinegar

3 medium potatoes, peeled and diced

1 (28-oz [800-g]) can basil and oregano crushed tomatoes, undrained

5 cups (1.2 L) vegetable broth (or 5 cups [1.2 L] water + 3 tbsp [18 g] vegetable bouillon powder)

1 tbsp (15 ml) agave nectar or honey (20 g), or more to taste

1 tsp salt, or more to taste

1 tsp dried basil

1 (15-oz [425-g]) can white cannellini beans, undrained

2½ cups (263 g) gluten-free short pasta

3 carrots, chopped

1 medium zucchini, diced

Freshly ground black pepper, to taste

Fresh basil, for garnish

Place your olive oil, onion, garlic, bay leaves, oregano, balsamic vinegar, potatoes, crushed tomatoes, broth, agave, salt, basil and beans in your Instant Pot. Close the lid and move the valve to SEALING. Use the PRESSURE button to set your Instant Pot to high pressure. Hit MANUAL and press the plus and minus buttons to reach 6 minutes.

Once the timer is done, move the valve to VENTING to quickly release the pressure. Open the lid and add the gluten-free pasta, carrots and zucchini.

Close the lid and move the valve to SEALING. Hit MANUAL and use the plus and minus buttons to reach 3 minutes.

Once the timer is done, move the valve to VENTING to quickly release the pressure and open the lid. Taste and adjust the salt and pepper to your liking. If it's too acidic, add a touch more agave or honey. Discard the bay leaves. Serve garnished with fresh basil.

Ham & No-Soak Bean Soup

Living right across from my grade school while growing up, I'd often walk home for lunch. A common meal was condensed ham and bean soup, especially because Idaho is frequently cold or chilly. Now, after having a from-scratch version that isn't a gelatinous glop that resembles the shape of a can when you pour it, I wonder how I did it and am grateful my taste buds matured. With the Instant Pot, dried beans quickly become velvety soft. The secret to a deep flavored broth is the ham hock—you can't skip it! Ask your butcher to help you find it.

SERVES 4 TO 6

1 lb (455 g) dried great northern beans, rinsed

6 cups (1.4 L) chicken broth (or 6 cups [1.4 L] water + ¼ cup [24 g] chicken bouillon powder)

2 cups (275 ml) water

1 ham hock

1 medium yellow onion, chopped

3 cloves garlic, minced (about 1½ tsp [4.5 g])

2 bay leaves

2 tsp (2 g) dried rosemary

2 cups (300 g) chopped ham

1 cup (130 g) diced carrot

2 medium potatoes, diced small

Salt and pepper, to taste

Place your beans, broth, water, ham hock, onion, garlic, bay leaves and rosemary in your Instant Pot. Close the lid and move the valve to SEALING. Use the PRESSURE button to set your Instant Pot to high pressure. Hit MANUAL and use the plus and minus buttons to reach 45 minutes.

Once the timer is done, move the valve to VENTING to quickly release the pressure. Pick out any shriveled beans that have floated to the top.

Add the ham, carrot and potatoes. Close the lid again and move the valve to SEALING. Hit MANUAL and use the plus and minus buttons to reach 5 minutes.

Once the timer is done, move the valve to VENTING to quickly release the pressure. Taste, and adjust the salt and pepper to your liking. Discard the bay leaves before serving.

No-Crust-Needed Pizza Soup

Making a vegan and gluten-free pizza crust from scratch, and then making the toppings, is an all-afternoon affair. It's expensive and time-consuming. I found I still craved the toppings but dreaded the work. This pizza soup gives me all the things I love: basil, green bell peppers, mushrooms, Italian sausage and pepperoni—all in an easy soup form. It's a combo pizza without so many carbs. This savory soup is the best of the soup and pizza worlds. Winning! I've found if you're using a good-quality gluten-free pasta made from a blend (for example ours is corn and brown rice), that this soup can freeze well, too!

SERVES 4 TO 6

1 tbsp (15 ml) olive oil

1 red onion, diced

1 lb (455 g) Italian sausage

1 (14-oz [400-g]) jar pizza sauce

56 oz (1.7 L) water (or 4 empty pizza sauce jarfuls of water)

1 green bell pepper, seeded and chopped

8 oz (225 g) mushrooms, sliced

1 (15-oz [425-g]) can diced tomatoes, undrained

8 oz (225 g) turkey pepperoni, sliced into quarters

1½ tsp (1 g) dried basil

1 tbsp (3 g) dried oregano

6 oz (170 g) gluten-free pasta (we like rotini)

OPTIONAL GARNISHES

Sliced black olives

Fresh basil

Hit the SAUTÉ function and pour your olive oil into your Instant Pot. Once it is hot (happens quickly!), add your onion and Italian sausage. Cook until the sausage is browned. Turn off your Instant Pot.

Next, add the rest of your ingredients: the pizza sauce, water, bell pepper, mushrooms, diced tomatoes, pepperoni, basil, oregano and pasta.

Close the lid and move the valve to SEALING. Use the PRESSURE button to set your Instant Pot to high pressure. Hit the MANUAL button and use the plus and minus buttons to reach 4 minutes.

Once the timer is done, move the valve to VENTING to quickly release the pressure. Once you can, open the lid, give everything a good stir and serve.

Top with garnishes, if so desired.

No-Red-Meat Chili

I am picky about my chili! I want it thick with a touch of heat, but not too hot since we can't rely on sour cream and cheese to tone it down. I want the texture to be robust, and it can't have red meat due to my son's beef allergy. Thankfully for me and you, I've come up with my all-time favorite chili recipe. Since I always make corn bread with it (my husband has taught me the magic of crumbling it on top), I've incorporated some cornmeal into the soup, which gives it extra texture. And the brown sugar gives it just a touch of sweetness. Be sure to serve this with a big bag of corn chips as we do (we like Fritos)! I prefer ground chicken, but ground turkey works here, too. Feel free to omit the Worcestershire sauce if your allergies prohibit it.

SERVES 4 TO 6

1 tbsp (15 ml) olive oil

1 lb (455 g) ground chicken

1 large red onion, chopped

1 (15-oz [425-g]) can kidney beans, drained

1 (15-oz [425-g]) can black beans, drained

1 (15-oz [425-g]) can pinto beans, drained

1 red bell pepper, seeded and chopped

½ jalapeño pepper, seeded and minced (optional)

2½ cups (590 ml) chicken or vegetable broth (or 2½ cups [590 ml] water + 5 tsp [7.5 g] bouillon powder)

⅓ cup (47 g) cornmeal

1 tbsp (7.5 g) chili powder

1½ tbsp (4.5 g) dried oregano

1½ tbsp (10.5 g) ground cumin

2½ tsp (16 g) kosher salt

1 tsp freshly ground black pepper

1½ tbsp (22.5 ml) gluten-free Worcestershire sauce

9 cloves garlic, minced (about 1½ tbsp [15 g])

1 tbsp (15 g) light brown sugar

1 (15-oz [425-g]) can diced fire-roasted tomatoes with juice

1 (6-oz [170-g]) can tomato paste

OPTIONAL GARNISHES

Dairy-free sour cream

Fresh cilantro

Lime wedges

Corn chips

Hit SAUTÉ and place your olive oil, ground chicken and red onion in your Instant Pot. Cook until the chicken is cooked through, for 5 to 7 minutes. Turn off your Instant Pot.

Place your kidney beans, black beans, pinto beans, bell pepper, jalapeño (if using), broth, cornmeal, chili powder, oregano, cumin, salt, pepper and Worcestershire in the Instant Pot.

Close the lid and move the valve to SEALING. Use the PRESSURE button to set your Instant Pot to high pressure. Hit MANUAL and use the plus and minus buttons to reach 20 minutes.

Once the timer is done, open the lid and stir in the garlic, brown sugar, tomatoes and tomato paste. Once everything is incorporated, serve with your choice of garnishes. This freezes wonderfully!

Ham & Corn Chowder

With the corn and ham, this ultimate mix of sweet and salty strikes a balance that will be hard to resist. Add to the fact that the soup utilizes bacon grease and is garnished with bacon for twice the pork and twice the flavor. I used to make this on the stovetop and waiting for the potatoes to cook felt like forever. I love how much quicker it is for this to get into my belly.

SERVES 4 TO 6

6 slices bacon

1 yellow onion, diced

1 lb (455 g) potatoes (4 or 5 small potatoes), diced into bite-size pieces

2½ cups (590 ml) water

2 tbsp (12 g) chicken bouillon powder

2 bay leaves

8 oz (225 g) ham, diced

1 tbsp (10 g) garlic, minced

1 tsp salt, or more to taste

2 (15-oz [425-g]) cans sweet corn, with liquid

1 cup (235 ml) canned full-fat coconut milk

Freshly ground black pepper, for garnish

Using kitchen shears, cut the bacon into bite-size pieces and place them in your Instant Pot. Hit SAUTÉ. Cook until the bacon is crisp, about 5 to 7 minutes. Transfer the bacon to a paper towel–lined plate. Add the onion and saute until soft and translucent, 1 to 2 minutes. Turn off the SAUTÉ function.

Remove all but 1 to 2 tablespoons (15 to 30 ml) of the bacon grease and add the potatoes, water, bouillon, bay leaves, ham, garlic, salt and corn to the Instant Pot.

Close the lid and move the valve to SEALING. Use the PRESSURE button to set your Instant Pot to high pressure. Hit MANUAL and use the plus and minus buttons to reach 7 minutes.

Once the timer is done, move the valve to VENTING to quickly release the pressure.

Open the lid, stir in the coconut milk and add back the bacon. Discard the bay leaves.

Adjust the salt to taste and top with pepper.

Creamy White Chicken Chili

Smooth and mild, this white chicken chili has light heat, a bite of sweet from the corn and a delicious white broth, thanks to rice milk and some dairy-free cream cheese. Best of all, the Instant Pot turns chicken icicles into tender shredded chicken with its pressurized magic. No chopping of vegetables required, as this is a pour, stir and forget about it kind of dinner.

SERVES 4 TO 6

2 frozen boneless, skinless chicken breasts (about 1 lb [455 g])

1 tbsp (15 ml) olive oil

1 tbsp (6 g) chicken bouillon powder

1½ tsp (4 g) chili powder

1 tsp ground cumin

1 tsp garlic salt

½ tsp onion powder

½ tsp freshly ground black pepper, or more to taste

½ tsp salt, or more to taste

½ tsp seasoned salt

Pinch of cayenne pepper (optional)

1½ cups (355 ml) water

1 (4-oz [115-g]) can chopped green chiles

1 (15-oz [425-g]) can corn, undrained

1 (15-oz [425-g]) can great northern beans, undrained

1 cup (235 ml) unsweetened rice milk

4 oz (115 g) dairy-free cream cheese

2 tbsp (16 g) cornstarch or arrowroot powder

TOPPINGS

Fresh cilantro, chopped

Tortilla chips, crushed

Place your frozen chicken, olive oil, bouillon, chili powder, cumin, garlic salt, onion powder, pepper, salt, seasoned salt, cayenne (if using), water, green chiles, corn and northern beans in your Instant Pot. Close the lid and move the valve to SEALING. Use the PRESSURE button to set your Instant Pot to high pressure. Hit MANUAL, and use the plus and minus buttons to reach 30 minutes.

While it cooks, place the rice milk, dairy-free cream cheese and cornstarch in a blender. Blend until the cream cheese is completely smooth, then set aside.

Once the timer is done, move the valve to VENTING to quickly release the pressure.

Open the lid of the Instant Pot, remove the chicken and shred it; then return the chicken to the pot.

Pour in the cheese mixture and stir to incorporate.

Taste and adjust the salt and black pepper to your liking. Serve with chopped fresh cilantro and crushed tortilla chips.

Chicken & Mexican Rice Soup

This tomato-based broth is anything but plain with green chiles and an entire bottle of salsa to impart tons of Southwest flavor. Tender shredded chicken, rice and beans make this one-bowl dinner filling and so satisfying. With the rice absorbing part of the liquid as it cooks, it's a cross between a soup and a casserole. Grab two frozen chicken breasts (no need to thaw!), dice an onion, measure the spices and pour the liquids in for a dinner that cooks in 30 minutes. From freezer to table—talk about a weeknight saver!

SERVES 4 TO 6

1 tbsp (15 ml) olive oil

2 frozen boneless, skinless chicken breasts (about 1 lb [455 g])

1 red onion, diced

1 (4.5-oz [130-g]) can diced green chiles

1 (16-oz [455-g]) jar mild salsa (or hotter if you enjoy more heat)

½ tsp salt

½ tsp ground cumin

½ tsp chili powder

½ tsp freshly ground black pepper

½ tsp dried oregano

5 cups (1.2 L) chicken broth (or 5 cups [1.2 L] water + 3 tbsp [18 g] chicken bouillon powder)

½ cup (98 g) uncooked white rice

1 (15-oz [425-g]) can black beans, drained and rinsed well

Fresh cilantro, chopped, for garnish

Tortilla chips, for garnish

Place your olive oil, chicken, onion, green chiles, salsa, salt, cumin, chili powder, pepper, oregano and broth in your Instant Pot. Close to the lid and move the valve to SEALING. Use the PRESSURE button to set your Instant Pot to high pressure. Hit MANUAL and use the plus and minus buttons to reach 25 minutes.

Once the timer is done, move the valve to VENTING to quickly release the pressure.

Open the lid and add the rice. Close the lid and move the valve to SEALING. Hit MANUAL and use the plus and minus buttons to reach 5 minutes.

When the timer is done, move the valve to VENTING to quickly release the pressure.

Open the lid and shred the chicken. Add the beans.

Stir well to incorporate everything. Ladle into bowls and top with fresh cilantro. Serve with tortilla chips.

Thai Coconut Soup

If you're sick of the same-ol', same-ol' soup, this will *definitely* get you out of your rut. With the unique flavors of ginger, lime and coconut milk, this Asian-inspired dish will shake away the doldrums. I put off making a soup like this for years, since I don't love Thai food in general, but that leap of faith was totally rewarded—so, if you're scared, take my hand and come with me to the land of flavor. My kids love the broth so much they drink that first because they just can't help themselves. You may find yourself in the same situation!

SERVES 4 TO 6

2 tbsp (30 ml) olive oil

1 tbsp (9 g) finely minced jalapeño pepper

1 tbsp (8 g) grated or finely diced fresh ginger

2 cloves garlic, minced (about 1 tsp)

3½ cups (830 ml) chicken broth (or 3½ cups [830 ml] water + 7 tsp [14 g] chicken bouillon powder)

½ tsp sriracha sauce (or more to taste)

1 tsp salt

2 chicken breasts (about 1 lb [455 g])

½ cup (35 g) chopped mushrooms

½ red bell pepper, sliced

8 oz (225 g) rice noodles (I like Thai Kitchen Stir-Fry Rice Noodles)

1 (13.5-oz [400-ml]) can full-fat coconut milk

¼ cup (60 ml) fresh lime juice

¼ cup (10 g) chopped fresh cilantro, for garnish

Place your olive oil, jalapeño, ginger, garlic, broth, sriracha, salt, chicken, mushrooms and bell pepper in your Instant Pot. Close the lid and move the valve to SEALING. Use the PRESSURE button to set your Instant Pot to high pressure. Hit MANUAL and use the plus and minus buttons to reach 25 minutes.

Once the timer is done, move the valve to VENTING to quickly release the pressure.

Open the lid and add the noodles. Close the lid again and move the valve to SEALING. Hit MANUAL and use the plus or minus buttons to reach 4 minutes.

Once the timer is done, move the valve to VENTING to quickly release the pressure.

Open the lid, stir in the coconut milk and lime juice, and separate any noodles that have stuck together.

Remove the chicken from the pot and shred, then return it to the pot.

Ladle into bowl and then top with the cilantro.

Cream-Free Tomato Bisque

I solemnly swear to never eat tomato soup from a can again. It would be a crime against my taste buds now that they've had this. I erroneously thought tomato soup was just for dipping allergy-safe grilled cheese into, but to my surprise and delight, I found myself drinking this as if it was nectar from the gods. The flavor was so rich and so deep that I had no problems polishing off the leftovers as well. It's also super easy because you can roughly chop the onion and celery and even keep the carrot whole. Since you'll just be pureeing it all, there's no hassle of finely dicing! Plus, did I mention . . . bacon?

SERVES 4 TO 6

6 slices bacon

1 sweet onion, roughly chopped

1 carrot, whole

1 celery rib, roughly chopped

5 cloves garlic, minced (about 2½ tsp [7.5 g])

5 cups (1.2 L) chicken broth (or 5 cups [1.2 L] water + 3 tbsp [18 g] chicken bouillon powder)

1 (28-oz [800-g]) can whole peeled tomatoes, undrained

1 tsp dried parsley

¼ tsp dried thyme

1 bay leaf

2 tsp (12.5 g) kosher salt, or more to taste

1 cup (235 ml) canned full-fat coconut milk, plus more for serving

Freshly ground black pepper, to taste

Using kitchen shears, cut the bacon into bite-size pieces and add them to your Instant Pot. Hit SAUTÉ and cook until the bacon is crisp, for 5 to 7 minutes. Transfer the bacon to a paper towel–lined plate, leaving the grease.

Add your onion, carrot, celery, garlic, broth, tomatoes, parsley, thyme, bay leaf and salt to the Instant Pot. Close the lid and move the valve to SEALING. Use the PRESSURE button to set your Instant Pot to high pressure. Hit the MANUAL button and use the plus and minus buttons to reach 10 minutes.

Once the timer is done, move the valve to VENTING to quickly release the pressure. Discard the bay leaf.

Open the lid and use an immersion blender or a high-quality blender to puree the mixture. This may take 2 to 3 batches, if using a blender.

Once everything is blended, stir in your coconut milk. Taste and adjust the salt and pepper to your liking.

Top with more coconut milk, if desired, and add the reserved bacon and additional pepper. Serve with allergy-safe grilled cheese or your favorite allergy-friendly bread, toasted with allergy-safe butter and garlic salt for dipping.

Homemade Bone Broth

While bone broths may be trending, this recipe actually started out of necessity because at one point my son couldn't have celery, and I couldn't find a store-bought version of broth that didn't include it. I used to make it on the stovetop and have it simmer overnight. It's so nice to only have to cook for 45 minutes now! You'll notice my broth is not clear—I like to make sure my kids get every ounce of nutrition they can, so I blend the vegetables into the broth. If you want a clear broth, you can strain out the vegetables with the bones.

SERVES 4 TO 6

Bones from 1 organic rotisserie chicken

1 yellow onion, roughly chopped

3 celery ribs, roughly chopped

6 cloves garlic, minced (about 1 tbsp [10 g])

1 tsp dried rosemary

1 tsp dried parsley

1 tsp dried thyme

1 tbsp (18 g) salt

2 bay leaves

10 to 12 cups (2.4 to 2.8 L) water

Place all your ingredients in your Instant Pot, making sure everything is submerged in the water (it's okay if some the bones are sticking out) and taking care not to go over the maximum fill line for your model.

Close the lid and move the valve to SEALING. Use the PRESSURE button to set your Instant Pot to high pressure. Hit MANUAL and use the plus and minus buttons to reach 45 minutes.

Once the timer is done, move the valve to VENTING to quickly release the pressure.

Remove and discard the bones and bay leaves. Using either an immersion blender or high-quality blender and working in batches, blend the vegetables and liquid, being careful of the hot soup.

Eat this soup within 2 to 3 days or freeze it for up to 6 months. This can be consumed plain or used as a base for all of my soups.

Chicken & (Rice) Noodle Soup

Were you starting to get nervous that my cookbook would have a soups section without chicken noodle? Never fear. I've saved one of my favorites (really—how can I choose?) for last. My oldest loves it so much, he'd eat it in the heat of summer. Perfect for days you feel sick—or any old day—this classic recipe tastes just as good, even with gluten-free noodles. And don't forget the bit of lemon at the end, as it helps all the flavors shine bright.

SERVES 4 TO 6

2 large frozen chicken breasts (about 1 lb [455 g])

1 tsp freshly ground black pepper, or more to taste

1 tbsp (15 ml) olive oil

1 large yellow onion, chopped

10 cups (2.4 L) chicken broth (or 10 cups [2.4 L] water + ⅓ cup [32 g] chicken bouillon powder)

3 bay leaves

¼ tsp dried thyme

1 tsp dried parsley

2 celery ribs, chopped

4 medium carrots, chopped

2½ cups (210 g) uncooked gluten-free rotini

1 tbsp (15 ml) fresh lemon juice

3 cloves garlic, minced (about 1½ tsp [4.5 g])

Salt, to taste

Place your chicken, pepper, olive oil, onion, broth, bay leaves, thyme and parsley in your Instant Pot. Close the lid and move the valve to SEALING. Use the PRESSURE button to set your Instant Pot to high pressure. Hit MANUAL and use the plus and minus buttons to reach 25 minutes.

When the timer is done, move the valve to VENTING to quickly release the pressure.

Open the lid and add the celery, carrots and gluten-free rotini. Close the lid. Move the valve back to SEALING. Hit MANUAL and use the plus and minus buttons to reach 3 minutes.

When the timer is done, move the valve to VENTING to quickly release the pressure.

Remove the chicken from the pot, shred it and return it to the pot. Add the lemon juice and garlic and stir well. Discard the bay leaves. Taste and adjust the salt and pepper to your liking.

Speedy Sweets

What would dinner be without a sweet note to end on? Dessert is my favorite part of the meal, and it's often the bribery that gets my kids to finish eating most nights. It's a lifesaver, quite frankly. It's my moment of indulgence for making it through a hectic and noisy day with my kids, and it's their reward for eating their vegetables. It's a win-win for the entire family.

While the Instant Pot is great at many things, I wouldn't recommend baking just anything in the there—trust me, I've tried. Here I've compiled five of the recipes it does best. And having an Instant Pot when it's summer sure makes baking desserts far more bearable than heating up your entire kitchen with your oven . . . because you'll seriously crave my Chocolate Pudding Cake with melty ice cream (page 131) this summer!

Baking a sweet treat that is free of wheat, dairy and eggs can be intimidating—but try this without an oven and you'll really impress! People will taste the Oat-Free Peach Cobbler (page 136) and think, *I didn't even smell it cooking in the oven!* It's almost as if you've made it out of thin air, you magical, allergy-baking goddess, you!

My family has *the* biggest sweet tooth, and it's always good to have a few go-to desserts up your sleeve to either satisfy your sugar craving, or for when company is over—especially something as impressive as my Dairy-Free Chocolate Fondue (page 132), which no one would guess is vegan!

My friend who recipe tested the Chocolate Mint Pudding (page 135) says I've ruined boxed mixes for her, so buyer beware! Do not try these desserts unless you're willing to expose your taste buds to some incredible finds.

Raspberry Orange Rice Pudding

In addition to making this without dairy milk, I decided to scrap the traditional flavors and add a fruitier twist. I am obsessed with raspberries, and a hint of orange just seemed like good measure. This is delicious on its own but absolutely *divine* with fresh berries and a little more coconut milk swirled on top. Make sure to get seedless raspberry jam to keep this smooth and creamy, as well as two cans of coconut milk for enough to finish the recipe!

SERVES 4 TO 6

1½ cups (355 ml) water

2 cups (470 ml) canned full-fat coconut milk (shaken before poured), divided

1 cup (195 g) uncooked basmati rice

Zest of 1 orange

¼ cup (60 g) light brown sugar

Pinch of salt

1 tsp ground cinnamon

2 tsp (10 ml) vanilla extract

½ cup (160 ml) seedless raspberry jam

Fresh berries, for serving (optional)

Place your water, 1 cup (235 ml) of the coconut milk and the rice, orange zest, brown sugar, salt, cinnamon and vanilla in your Instant Pot. Close the lid and move the valve to SEALING. Use the PRESSURE button to set your Instant Pot to high pressure. Hit the MANUAL button and use the plus and minus buttons to reach 5 minutes.

Once the timer is done, allow it to naturally release for 10 minutes. Once the display shows "L:10," move the valve to VENTING to finish releasing any leftover pressure.

Open the lid and stir in the remaining cup (235 ml) of coconut milk and the raspberry jam. I like mine thick, but feel free to add more coconut milk if you prefer a thinner consistency.

Serve warm or cold, with additional drizzles of coconut milk to your preference. Best if served with fresh berries on top.

Chocolate Pudding Cake

It's a pudding, it's a cake . . . it's a chocolate pudding cake! A fun mix of two of our favorite desserts, this sticky chocolate cake has an underbelly of pudding that is thick and gooey and absolutely chocolatey. Don't hate me for using a total of 3½ cups (790 g) of brown sugar—be sure you have plenty before you start. The cake wanted that much brown sugar, so I listened to the cake. This is an allergy-friendly cookbook, but definitely not a diet one! I am often asked, "If you don't need to be gluten-free, can you swap out regular flour one to one?" The answer is yes, and simply omit the xanthan gum. This is one of my husband's favorite cakes, but we need help settling a disagreement: which dairy-free ice cream do you like to top it with, vanilla or mint chip? (I say mint chip!)

SERVES 4 TO 6

CAKE BATTER

Nonstick flour-free cooking spray

2 cups (450 g) light brown sugar

2 cups (250 g) gluten-free flour (see my blog for my preferred blend)

6 tbsp (42 g) unsweetened cocoa powder

4 tsp (18 g) baking powder

1 tsp salt

½ tsp xanthan gum (omit if your gluten-free flour already has this in the blend)

1 cup (235 ml) rice milk

¼ cup (60 ml) coconut oil, melted

1 tsp vanilla extract

PUDDING

1½ cups (340 g) light brown sugar

½ cup (55 g) unsweetened cocoa powder

3 cups (710 ml) boiling water

Dairy-free vanilla or mint chip ice cream, for serving

Grease your Instant Pot bowl well along the bottom and sides with nonstick cooking spray.

In a large mixing bowl, whisk together your brown sugar, gluten-free flour, cocoa powder, baking powder, salt and xanthan gum, if using. Stir to remove any clumps.

Next, pour in the rice milk, coconut oil and vanilla. Stir until everything is combined.

Pour this into the prepared bowl of your Instant Pot.

To make the pudding, in the same mixing bowl, whisk together the brown sugar and cocoa powder. Evenly spread this dry mixture over the wet cake mixture in the Instant Pot.

Pour the boiling water directly on top of the cake.

Close the lid and move the valve to SEALING. Use the PRESSURE button to set your Instant Pot to high pressure. Hit MANUAL and use the plus and minus buttons to reach 35 minutes.

Once the timer is done, move the valve to VENTING to quickly release the pressure. The cake will be mostly set on top, with gooeyness underneath from the pudding.

Serve warm with your favorite dairy-free ice cream on top to cut the richness of the cake.

Dairy-Free Chocolate Fondue

Spice up your typical dessert with this self-serve option. The Instant Pot provides the perfect double boiler to melt your chocolate, and using coconut milk in place of cream still allows the chocolate to shine through. The ultimate topping for just about any sliced fruit, marshmallows, gluten-free pretzels or even chopped-up crispy rice squares (see my blog for the recipe!). Great for holidays or even date nights in. I love to use Enjoy Life brand chocolate chips for my vegan chocolate; in fact, I prefer a combination of semisweet and dark chocolate so that it's not so rich. If you're a dark chocolate lover, feel free to use all dark. For fun twists, you can also add other extracts to spice it up. Orange or peppermint would be fun around the holidays!

SERVES 4 TO 6

1 cup (235 ml) water

5 oz (140 g) vegan semisweet chocolate chips

5 oz (140 g) vegan dark chocolate chips

¼ cup (60 ml) rice milk

⅓ cup (80 ml) canned full-fat coconut milk

1 tsp vanilla extract

LOTS OF DIPPING OPTIONS:

Apples

Pineapples

Strawberries

Bananas

Marshmallows

Gluten-free dairy-free pretzels

Crispy rice cereal

Pour the water into the bottom of your Instant Pot. Place all the chocolate chips, rice milk and coconut milk in a glass bowl large enough to sit on the Instant Pot without falling in.

Hit SAUTÉ to bring the water to a boil while frequently stirring the chocolate mixture with a heatproof spatula or wooden spoon.

Once the chocolate is completely melted—it only takes a few minutes—turn off the Instant Pot and carefully remove the bowl using oven mitts. Stir in the vanilla.

Serve immediately or pour into a fondue warmer. For leftovers, simply reheat with a little more coconut milk.

Chocolate Mint Pudding

Move over, Jell-O! My pudding has a velvety, melt-in-your-mouth texture and a rich chocolate taste. One of my favorite combos is chocolate and mint, so I couldn't leave this as just plain chocolate pudding. Feel free to omit the mint extract if you'd prefer regular chocolate. Simply pour the ingredients in the Instant Pot and whisk; the cornstarch and heat will set up the rest for you. Once you realize how simple from-scratch pudding is, you may be making this all of the time!

SERVES 4 TO 6

¼ cup (28 g) unsweetened cocoa powder

¼ cup (32 g) cornstarch or arrowroot powder

½ cup (100 g) sugar

Pinch of salt

1 (13.5-oz [400-ml]) can full-fat coconut milk

1 cup (235 ml) rice milk

¼ cup (44 g) vegan semisweet chocolate chips

¼ cup (44 g) vegan dark chocolate chips

1½ tsp (7.5 ml) mint extract

Fresh mint sprigs, for garnish (optional)

Dairy-free whipped topping, for garnish (optional)

Place your cocoa powder, cornstarch, sugar and salt in your Instant Pot. Whisk well to combine and work out any clumps from the cocoa.

Next, add the coconut milk and rice milk. Whisk until everything is incorporated.

Then, set your Instant Pot to SAUTÉ. Whisk occasionally until the mixture reaches a full boil—be careful, you don't want it to scorch. Once it's boiling, turn off the Instant Pot. Stir vigorously for 1 more minute.

Take the insert out of the Instant Pot and stir in all the chocolate chips and the mint extract until the chocolate is completely melted. Pour into serving glasses. Place in the fridge until the pudding is cool or until ready to serve. Keep the rest of the pudding covered in an airtight container for 1 to 2 days.

Garnish with fresh mint and dairy-free whipped topping, if so desired.

Oat-Free Peach Cobbler

If you're like us and can't do oats—not even gluten-free oats—it makes traditional fruit desserts, such as cobblers, a bit difficult. I figured out a great crisp topping that uses a cake box mix to make life even simpler! I also incorporated canned peaches instead of fresh so you can enjoy this all year long, because sometimes you just need a good peach cobbler with melty vanilla ice cream.

SERVES 2 TO 3

2 cups (475 ml) water

1 (8-oz [225-g]) can peaches, juice drained

1 cup (125 g) gluten- and dairy-free yellow cake mix (I use Walmart brand)

¼ cup (60 ml) melted coconut oil

½ tsp vanilla extract

½ tsp ground cinnamon

Dairy-free vanilla ice cream, for serving (optional)

Dairy-free whipped topping, for serving (optional)

Place the water in your Instant Pot. Set the trivet on top of the water. Place the drained peaches in a small cake pan that can fit inside the Instant Pot (I use one that's 6 inches [15 cm] in diameter).

In a small bowl, combine the cake mix, coconut oil, vanilla and cinnamon. Stir until everything is incorporated and it resembles a fine crumb.

Evenly sprinkle the crumble on top of the peaches. Cover the cake pan tightly with aluminum foil. Place the cake pan on the trivet.

Use the PRESSURE button to set your Instant Pot to high pressure. Hit MANUAL and use the plus and minus buttons to reach 10 minutes.

Once the timer is done, move the valve to VENTING and quickly release the pressure.

With oven mitts, carefully lift the cake pan out of the Instant Pot. Being careful of the steam, remove the aluminum foil. Serve the cobbler either plain, a dairy-free vanilla ice cream or a dairy-free whipped topping.

TIP: Be sure to read the box mix ingredients. Several gluten-free box mixes have powdered milk in them.

Acknowledgments

To my parents, Brent and Kelli Egbert, who have always been my cheerleaders. For my mom, who prepared a home-cooked meal for me every day while I was growing up—plus you almost always had a delicious snack waiting for us after school—I'm still trying to fill your motherly shoes! Thank you for showing me the gift of the consistent nightly sit-down dinners. For my dad, who constantly goes to my site and watches every video I make.

To my best friends, Alicia, Stacey, Whitney and Yesenia, for their advice, help with picking photos and never-ending support. Your brainstorming, listening to me vent on endless Marco Polos, phone calls and texts fuel me with ideas and love. You'll never know the deep meaning I get from your validating friendships.

To my sweet husband, Claudy, who has never complained when I've had flops in the kitchen, eats my leftovers, watches the kids whenever I take too much on, never tells me no when I have an idea, never questions when I say something is going to cost us money and encourages me to dream even bigger. Thank you for allowing me to fly and providing a safe nest for when I fall.

To my children:

> To Carter—your life changing diagnoses have pushed my culinary boundaries, making me a better cook than I probably ever would have been without them, helping me to be more aware of what I eat and teaching me to be healthier. While often hard—I'm sure it's put years on all of our lives—I'd spend days in the kitchen just to hear you tell me something is delicious and to know that you're healthy. Thank you for being such a brave boy and being so resilient about your medical issues.

> To Calvin—seeing you get excited about food has to be the most organic, authentic excitement there is in the world. Your ability to sniff out an ounce of sugar that I have hidden in the house never ceases to baffle me. I love hearing you say something "smelly yummy" and to hear your excruciatingly honest, yet sweet, voice exclaim something tastes good!

> To Kennedy—at only one year old, you are already a joy to feed. I look forward to many mom-and-daughter food dates. Please always give me that big grin when we sit down to eat together, where you tilt your chin upward! May I never forget that look.

To my recipe testers, Alicia, Gianna, Grandma, Juli, Molly and Scott, thank you for taking my recipes into your kitchens. Your feedback and help was so appreciated.

To my mom and Keri, who watched my kids for hours and hours while I made this cookbook: Seriously, my mom is going straight to heaven.

To Tyson, I know you're proud. You're never forgotten. May I cook for you someday in heaven.

To my awesome readers, you keep me wanting to produce recipe after recipe for you. It is a joy to share recipes with people who "get it" both here and on my blog.

To anyone and everyone who has ever had to cut out a food from their diet—I send you love and understanding.

To Page Street Publishing, especially Caitlin and Meg, thank you for finding me and asking me to do this. It felt as if the call came straight from heaven, and it has been the most pleasant surprise and thrill to put this together and see my name in print. Thank you for making this possible!

To God, may life's curveballs and tests always be something that refines me with Your help and grace. I know all of life's trials are boiling water—may I be carrots and not eggs. Not only are eggs allergic to our family, but I want to become soft and not hard when faced with challenges. I recognize everything good in my life comes from Thee.

About the Author

Megan created the blog allergyawesomeness.com in the fall of 2015, and it perfectly blends all of her passions: food, advocacy, photography and video. Megan's tenacity in researching and testing recipes and her unwillingness to eat bland foods the rest of her life has led her to many culinary successes. She loves to bring awareness, kindness and advocacy to those who suffer with food allergies. Her realness, openness and empathy have helped her fans—both newly adjusting to food allergies and other veteran allergy moms—feel connected and supported.

For several years, she sat on the board of a nonprofit focused on food allergies and handled the organization's PR.

Megan loves to write and often freelances, but her true love is still TV from her broadcast journalism days, and her favorite part of blogging is doing live television cooking segments. She is a dishwashing hater, but loves to dance in the kitchen, plan family outings, talk to her friends, serve in her church, snowboard when she can, be silly with her kids and eat desserts late at night. She lives in Utah with her husband, Claudy, and three beautiful children.

You can follow Megan on social media at:

Facebook.com/AllergyAwesomeness
Instagram.com/allergy_awesomeness
Pinterest.com/allergyawesome

Index

A

American Academy of Allergy, Asthma & Immunology (AAAAI), 8

anaphylaxis, 6

Apricot-Glazed Pork Chops, 51

asparagus: Two-Minute Lemon Asparagus, 92

B

baby corn: No-Stir Stir-Fry, 12

bacon

Bacon & Brown Sugar Baked Beans, 80

Cream-Free Zuppa Toscana, 96

Smothered Pork Chops, 60

beans

Bacon & Brown Sugar Baked Beans, 80

Chicken & Mexican Rice Soup, 116

Cilantro, Garlic & Lime Rice & Beans, 64

Creamy White Chicken Chili, 115

Ham & No-Soak Bean Soup, 107

No-Red-Meat Chili, 111

No-Soak Red Beans & Rice, 40

Potato & Sausage Soup, 100

Quinoa Nachos, 27

Sesame-Free Hummus, 83

Southwest Black Beans, 79

Thick & Creamy Refried Beans, 84

Tuscan White Bean Quinoa Salad, 35

Vegan & Gluten-Free Minestrone, 104

bell peppers

Creamy Rice-Milk Cajun Chicken Pasta, 44

No-Crust-Needed Pizza Soup, 108

No-Stir Stir-Fry, 12

Shellfish-Free Jambalaya, 43

Thai Coconut Soup, 119

Tuscan White Bean Quinoa Salad, 35

black beans

Chicken & Mexican Rice Soup, 116

Cilantro, Garlic & Lime Rice & Beans, 64

No-Red-Meat Chili, 111

Quinoa Nachos, 27

Southwest Black Beans, 79

black-eyed peas: Shellfish-Free Jambalaya, 43

Bone Broth, Homemade, 123

broccoli

Broccoli & "Cheese," 88

Honey Garlic Chicken & Broccoli, 15

Sweet & Tangy Pineapple Chicken, 16

C

Cake, Chocolate Pudding, 131

carrots

35-Minute Herb Crusted Turkey Breast, 48

Broccoli & "Cheese," 88

Chicken & (Rice) Noodle Soup, 124

Ham & No-Soak Bean Soup, 107

Honey Cinnamon Carrots, 87

No-Butter Indian "Butter" Chicken, 20

Shellfish-Free Jambalaya, 43

Vegan, Nut- & Gluten-Free Mac 'n' Cheese, 59

Vegan & Gluten-Free Minestrone, 104

cashew milk, 8

cauliflower: Healthier-for-You Orange Chicken, 19

chicken

Chicken & (Rice) Noodle Soup, 124

Chicken & Mexican Rice Soup, 116

Chicken Taco Salad, 56

Chili Lime Chicken Tacos, 24

Creamy Italian Chicken & Pasta, 36

Creamy Rice-Milk Cajun Chicken Pasta, 44

Creamy White Chicken Chili, 115

Greek Lemon Chicken & Potatoes, 39

Green Chile Chicken Enchilada Soup, 103

Healthier-for-You Orange Chicken, 19

Homemade Bone Broth, 123

Honey Garlic Chicken & Broccoli, 15

No-Butter Indian "Butter" Chicken, 20

No-Cans-Needed Chicken & Wild Rice Soup, 99

No-Red-Meat Chili, 111

No-Stir Stir-Fry, 12

Sweet & Tangy Pineapple Chicken, 16

Thai Coconut Soup, 119

chicken bouillon, 28

chickpeas. See garbanzo beans

chilies: Green Chile Chicken Enchilada Soup, 103

chili

Creamy White Chicken Chili, 115

No-Red-Meat Chili, 111

chocolate

Chocolate Mint Pudding, 135

Chocolate Pudding Cake, 131

Dairy-Free Chocolate Fondue, 132

Chowder, Ham & Corn, 112

coconut milk, 8

Chocolate Mint Pudding, 135

Raspberry Orange Rice Pudding, 128

Thai Coconut Soup, 119

corn

Creamy White Chicken Chili, 115

Easiest Corn on the Cob, 91

Ham & Corn Chowder, 112

cow's milk, 8

cranberries: Wild Rice, Cranberry & Sweet Potato Pilaf, 75

D

desserts

Chocolate Mint Pudding, 135

Chocolate Pudding Cake, 131

Dairy-Free Chocolate Fondue, 132

Oat-Free Peach Cobbler, 136

Raspberry Orange Rice Pudding, 128

dips and spreads

Sesame-Free Hummus, 83

Thick & Creamy Refried Beans, 84

E

eggs, 8

eosinophilic esophagitis (EOE), 6

F

fish, 8

Fondue, Dairy-Free Chocolate, 132

food allergies, 6

G

garbanzo beans: Sesame-Free Hummus, 83

H

ham

Ham & Corn Chowder, 112

Ham & No-Soak Bean Soup, 107

Honey Cinnamon Carrots, 87

Honey Garlic Chicken & Broccoli, 15

Hummus, Sesame-Free, 83

I

ingredients, 8

Instant Pot®, 7, 9

J

Jambalaya, Shellfish-Free, 43

K

kale: Cream-Free Zuppa Toscana, 96

kidney beans. See beans

M

meatballs: Bread Crumb– & Egg-Free Italian Meatballs & Spaghetti, 32

meat tenderness, 9

mushrooms

35-Minute Herb Crusted Turkey Breast, 48

Creamy Italian Chicken & Pasta, 36

No-Cans-Needed Chicken & Wild Rice Soup, 99

No-Cheese-Needed Ragu, 31

No-Crust-Needed Pizza Soup, 108

Shellfish-Free Jambalaya, 43

Smothered Pork Chops, 60

Thai Coconut Soup, 119

N

Nachos, Quinoa, 27

noodles. See pasta; rice noodles

O

orange

Healthier-for-You Orange Chicken, 19

Raspberry Orange Rice Pudding, 128

P

pasta

Bread Crumb– & Egg-Free Italian Meatballs & Spaghetti, 32

Chicken & (Rice) Noodle Soup, 124

Creamy Italian Chicken & Pasta, 36

Creamy Rice-Milk Cajun Chicken Pasta, 44

No-Cheese-Needed Ragu, 31

No-Crust-Needed Pizza Soup, 108

Vegan, Nut- & Gluten-Free Mac 'n' Cheese, 59

Vegan & Gluten-Free Minestrone, 104

peaches: Oat-Free Peach Cobbler, 136

peanuts, 8

peas

Creamy Italian Chicken & Pasta, 36

No-Stir Stir-Fry, 12

Shellfish-Free Jambalaya, 43

pineapple: Sweet & Tangy Pineapple Chicken, 16

pinto beans. See beans

pork

See also bacon; ham; sausage

Apricot-Glazed Pork Chops, 51

Classic Sunday Roast, 55

Dripping Balsamic Pork Roast, 47

Smothered Pork Chops, 60

Sun-Dried Tomato and Greek Herbed Roast, 52

Sweet Barbacoa, 23

Tomatillo Pork Tacos, 28

potatoes

Broccoli & "Cheese," 88

Cheese-Free Scalloped Potatoes, 72

Cream-Free Zuppa Toscana, 96

Dairy-Free Garlic Parsley Mashed Potatoes, 71

Greek Lemon Chicken & Potatoes, 39

Ham & Corn Chowder, 112

Ham & No-Soak Bean Soup, 107

Potato & Sausage Soup, 100

Vegan, Nut- & Gluten-Free Mac 'n' Cheese, 59

Vegan & Gluten-Free Minestrone, 104

pudding

Chocolate Mint Pudding, 135

Chocolate Pudding Cake, 131

Raspberry Orange Rice Pudding, 128

Q

quick release, 9

quinoa

Lemon Herbed Quinoa, 67

Quinoa Nachos, 27

Tuscan White Bean Quinoa Salad, 35

R

ragu sauce: No-Cheese-Needed Ragu, 31

Raspberry Orange Rice Pudding, 128

rice

Chicken & Mexican Rice Soup, 116

Cilantro, Garlic & Lime Rice & Beans, 64

No-Cans-Needed Chicken & Wild Rice Soup, 99

No-Soak Red Beans & Rice, 40

Salsa Mexican Rice, 68

Shellfish-Free Jambalaya, 43

Wild Rice, Cranberry & Sweet Potato Pilaf, 75

rice milk, 8

rice noodles, 32

Chicken & (Rice) Noodle Soup, 124

Creamy Italian Chicken & Pasta, 36

No-Stir Stir-Fry, 12

Thai Coconut Soup, 119

Rice Pudding, Raspberry Orange, 128

S

salads

Chicken Taco Salad, 56

Tuscan White Bean Quinoa Salad, 35

sauces: No-Cheese-Needed Ragu, 31

sausage

Bread Crumb– & Egg-Free Italian Meatballs & Spaghetti, 32

Cream-Free Zuppa Toscana, 96

Creamy Rice-Milk Cajun Chicken Pasta, 44

No-Cheese-Needed Ragu, 31

No-Crust-Needed Pizza Soup, 108

No-Soak Red Beans & Rice, 40

Potato & Sausage Soup, 100

Shellfish-Free Jambalaya, 43

shellfish, 8

Shellfish-Free Jambalaya, 43

soups

Chicken & (Rice) Noodle Soup, 124

Chicken & Mexican Rice Soup, 116

Cream-Free Tomato Bisque, 120

Cream-Free Zuppa Toscana, 96

Green Chile Chicken Enchilada Soup, 103

Ham & Corn Chowder, 112

Ham & No-Soak Bean Soup, 107

Homemade Bone Broth, 123

No-Cans-Needed Chicken & Wild Rice Soup, 99

No-Crust-Needed Pizza Soup, 108

Potato & Sausage Soup, 100

Thai Coconut Soup, 119

Vegan & Gluten-Free Minestrone, 104

soy, 8

spaghetti

Bread Crumb– & Egg-Free Italian Meatballs & Spaghetti, 32

No-Cheese-Needed Ragu, 31

spinach: Cream-Free Zuppa Toscana, 96

stir fries: No-Stir Stir-Fry, 12

Sun-Dried Tomato and Greek Herbed Roast, 52

sweet potatoes

Dairy-Free Sweet Potato Casserole, 76

Wild Rice, Cranberry & Sweet Potato Pilaf, 75

T

tacos

Chicken Taco Salad, 56

Chili Lime Chicken Tacos, 24

Tomatillo Pork Tacos, 28

Thai Coconut Soup, 119

Tomatillo Pork Tacos, 28

tomatoes

Bread Crumb– & Egg-Free Italian Meatballs & Spaghetti, 32

Cream-Free Tomato Bisque, 120

No-Cheese-Needed Ragu, 31

No-Crust-Needed Pizza Soup, 108

No-Red-Meat Chili, 111

Shellfish-Free Jambalaya, 43

Tuscan White Bean Quinoa Salad, 35

tree nuts, 8

turkey: 35-Minute Herb Crusted Turkey Breast, 48

turkey pepperoni: No-Crust-Needed Pizza Soup, 108

W

water chestnuts: No-Stir Stir-Fry, 12

wheat, 8

white beans

Creamy White Chicken Chili, 115

Green Chile Chicken Enchilada Soup, 103

Potato & Sausage Soup, 100

Tuscan White Bean Quinoa Salad, 35

Vegan & Gluten-Free Minestrone, 104

Wild Rice, Cranberry & Sweet Potato Pilaf, 75

Z

zucchini: Vegan & Gluten-Free Minestrone, 104